BOUTS IN EURO

Travel Poems

Harrison Abbott

ALSO BY HARRISON ABBOTT

NOVELS

Amazed Gloom

Filippo's Game

Polly's Dreams

Magpie Glen

Fox and the Birch Trees

Tannahills

A Trade of Grace

Down in Boxbush

Little Waterfall

SHORT STORIES

One Hundred Ticks

PART ONE – COUNTRIES FROM MEMORY

POLAND

I haven't been there in such a long time but
For some reason I still think about one
Particular image that reminds of the nation.
The strawberry kiosks on the street corners.
Folks selling fresh strawberries on the ends
Of the roads, and the blood red intensity of
The berries ... And, the ironical mix of the
Alcohol shops dotted around the streets, mixed,
Almost door to door, with the pharmacy shops.
So, you would see the neon lights of the alcohol
Stores in one place and then twenty yards down
The street there would be the green neon beam
Of an APTEKA sign. Health and poison aligned.
But there are far many other visions and memorial
Content, too. It's just that they are swirled up
In a type of dreamland that I rarely want to
Go back to, because I miss this country so much,
And the person that I used to visit there with –
I miss her as horrifically as any mental pain
I can fathom in my writing. But, I
Suppose that, via writing about this country,
It can be therapeutic. And so here goes.
The city I spent the most time in was Lodz.
A huge town with a population of around
700 000 people. And we would head through
The city on the wasp coloured trams that
Dinged and danged with their bells, along
The streets that were often filled with weeds
And under the tall buildings that were often
Left cracked and dilapidated. Sometimes
Because nobody was living in them and
Other times because they were still in ruins
From the war. And, on so many walls nearby
That you glanced, there was football graffiti.
Or, other slogans that I didn't know the
Origin of. Whenever you walked out on the
Street you were aware of high rises in the
Distance. Some folks find them ugly but I've
Always found them pretty in an off key way.
Those were hard fat bulky Soviet buildings
Of concrete that yomped up way high in the
Sky and there must've been hundreds of
People living in each domino set that you

Looked at: and they were dazed and delirious
In the central European sun. We would
Ride out to the outer parts of the city and
The flats would just go on and on into the
Distance. And whenever we rode on the trams or
On the train it always took thirty minutes to get
Anywhere – the town was that huge. Industrial.
We went to museums of textile works, ex-factories.
There was the sense that this city was one of
Working people, of GDP, of output. And yet it
Was still obliterated, in a way, by world war,
Even in the first quarter of the 21st century.
We went to the Jewish cemetery, far, far away
From where we were staying. And it remains
One of the largest cemeteries in Europe.
For reasons that I don't need to explain.
And most of the graveyards were surrounded by
Lofty trees in full bloom. Was a sunny day
When we went there. And the graves weren't
Proper graves. They were merely little
Placards that stung meekly out of the soil,
And most of them didn't have names. Just bodies,
Under the earth. Skeletons. ... And, my girl
And I went travelling out of Lodz a lot, too,
Between Warsaw and Opole and Krakow.
Thus, I witnessed much of the dense countryside
Between the cities. And the fields were rich
And lush and they almost didn't belong to the
Hard urbanity of the towns. There were still
Houses by the farms, but most of it was a series
Of long landscaped fields, flat and hazed in blue,
Yellow and hooker's green. ... And I remember
One time walking with her and her parents,
And her mother said, "There was a great battle
Here, back in the war. Against the Nazis."
And, we were literally just walking through
This angelic countryside. It was surreal
To hear her mention the Nazis so casually.
That they had been on this very turf,
70 years earlier, with their Blitzkrieg rage.
Her mother and father spoke only in English
To me; but I tried a few times with Polish,
And they found it funny, because my accent
Was so awful. But, when they were all speaking
In their own tongue, I liked the sound of their
Language and how it crashed and thrashed

With noises I couldn't understand. It had
A rough, clumsy, dance-like quality to it:
That Slavic thing that I wished I knew how to
Speak. But there was very little chance,
Considering all of their cases, and so on.
Or, maybe I wasn't smart enough to learn it
Properly. ... But in those summers, too, there
Were the football tournaments. And, because
Polska are usually a decent football team,
They were often involved in the competitions.
This was unusual for me, since I come
From Scotland. And so the city squares and
The main streets would be filled with folks
Wearing soccer shirts, and there would be huge
Public TV screens; and there was steaming pierogi,
And gaudy piwo [which is always high strength
In Poland, no matter which brand you pick]
And there would be an eruption whenever
There was a goal. Even though it was unlikely
That Poland would win the tournament it
Was still glorious to be involved.
When the games were over we would head
Elsewhere in the city and sit by the thick river and
Dabble at those intense beers. Yeah, I remember
Being in Warsaw by the Vistula and it was
Maybe eight in the evening and still piping
Hot and Poland was still throbbing and pulsing
With hundreds of other folks lacing the steps
By the bankside. The nation had been through
So much mayhem throughout its history,
And yet it was still here: there was a whole
Generation here by the banks of this mammoth
River: and even though I was a foreigner,
I still felt a part of the generation.
No, I wasn't Slavic: but I loved this nation indeed.

CYPRUS

I remember an immediate sense of quiet
When we stepped off the plane, onto the
Baked tarmac of the airport skirts: and
Even though it was an airport there was
A sense of hushed heat, and the sun was
A sheen of gold across the eyes, with
Sharp shadows whenever a building
Cracked through the rays. We went there
From Poland, and it was one of those
Package-holidays; so we got on a bus
Which took us to the hotel where we were
All staying: and thus I had the constant
Buzz of Polish all around me.
Paphos – was the place we went to.
The bus sailed over hilly lands, where,
Looking out, there was a dry, orange
Land, peppered with dark green bushes.
And by the time we got to the hotel it
Definitely seemed like a completely
Different world. We were right by the
Coast, and there was an airy sense of
The sea idling whenever you breathed.
We went down to the Mediterranean, and
Went into the water and it was like stepping
Into a warm bath, and, one could look out on
The horizon and realise why so many
Folks of history were inspired to sail out
On this most fantastic of seas: there was
Something mythical and tantalising about
The span of the turquoise water that drew
You in.
And, we would go for walks along the beaches
And up into the desert-like country, where
Lizards would scurry by the dusty roadsides,
Under the orange trees that grew naturally
With their shiny fruits. And there were the
Palm trees that shook when a breeze came
With dry crackling. And we would sit on
The balcony at night, which overlooked
A jumble of shops and bars the far side of
The road, which kept their pink and silver
Lights on throughout the night, and as we
Drank the cheap wine from the local store

They all washed together in a washy trance.
And, I've always been a night owl, so I
Would go out and explore the hotel when it
Was dark, and sit in the downstairs atrium
And read books in the bar that was open until
Four a.m. and there was a polite curtly-haired
Woman who worked there who I still recall
Strongly for some reason.
I stayed in that hotel for a full week and though
That's a short amount of time, when you live
In one place for seven days it can stamp
Imprints of beauty on your mind, and you
Will miss the place for the rest of your life
Because you know that you're never going
Back there. I've written stories based on
That place before, as a means to try and
Re-live (or forget?) the memories of it.
But, I guess, that is what grief is for: that you
Wouldn't be able to grieve if you'd never
Experienced the content in the first place.
But, yes, wandering about that hotel with
Its echoey corridors and the quaint electrics,
And writing stories on the tiny desk in our
Room, at night: they were glorious times.
And, the cats! I should have mentioned them
Already. Stray cats. Everywhere you looked
There would be a cat sneaking about with
Their feline charisma. There were two
Of them who would flirt with our room,
Because there was a rooftop just below
The balcony, and so they would come in
Through the patio doors. One was this
Fluffy female cat and the other was this
Slick male cat. And, my girl gave nicknames
For them both. I wonder whether those
Animals are still alive? Since I'm writing
This eight years after I went to Paphos. I
Hope they are. ... And, my girl was a slender,
Tall young lady with huge eyes, freckles
And hair that stretched down almost to
Her waist. I learned the contours of her
Body and listened to the stories from her
Youth and told her my ones too.
In my diary/journal I would draw pictures
Of her, alongside the writings and the
Notes I made. And I remember reading

A Margaret Atwood novel called
Oryx and Crake. That was the first of hers
That I read. And so that wacky sci fi book
Gave an extra surreal element to my
Entire time in Cyprus. ... In short, the whole
Country was one of intense, compact beauty.
As I'm writing now, in Edinburgh, Scotland:
There's a window just above me, and it's
Raining heavily, and there are white skies above.
And, I think of Cyprus as this never ending
Window vision – of a different kind. When I
Recall that place it is like looking through a window
Of a scene that never changes, of an ultramarine
Sky, and the effluvium of the sea nearby,
Of the sand and the sapped roads and the tiny
Stuffy shops where we bought bags of crisps
And small glass bottles of beer and packs of
Cigarettes without famous logos.
We hired bikes and we rode along the streets
And got to the district of the 'posh' hotels,
That were taller and fancier than our 3-Star one.
But, even though they were plush, they also seemed
Lost, on this island. Like they didn't belong
To commerce. And though they were big, there
Weren't many people about. They just seemed
Like pictures of hotels – like flourished postcard
Covers – rather than buildings were people were
Living in. And, at night, they would glow in the
Distance, with hues and shapes like torchlight
Shone through balloons. And often when we
Cycled in the evenings there were no cars
At all on the roads, and it was almost as if it
Was just she and I in this mini world – like
Riding about an empty town with only us
As the temporary inhabitants. But, eventually,
The seventh night came, and we got back on the
Bus with the rest of the Polish folks, to take us away.
Despite it being eight years: I've never written
Personally about Cyprus before. It comes up in
My fiction but not in a biographical sense. Maybe
I was postponing it, all this time, for some reason.
As I say, I won't be going back there ever again.
It wouldn't be the same. And, sometimes it's
Just better to leave a place for how you remember
It, even if the memories are painful to reconcile.

LONDON

I touched down at Stanstead at seven a.m.
Then got the train into the city, and thus I
Passed the provincial towns in the Metropolitan
Area where around an extra 6 million people
Live, towns which technically aren't part of the
Great capital. ... Lots of people I know totally
Hate London. Whenever I go there I'm
Astounded by its sheer scale and mania,
And, I'll admit, I always reap exhilaration when
I visit. ... I got off at Liverpool Street and
I went wandering about. I went to see
William Blake's grave. Which isn't in a proper
Cemetery, per se: it's quite an odd grave in
That it's just off the street, and built over with
Concrete. Then there is just his name,
With his bones somewhere underneath, and
I remember the immense sound of *drilling*:
As some men were working on a building
Site nearby, and it was as if 21st century
London was nothing like anything in a
William Blake poem. After that I found the
Nearest subway station, and went down
Into the tunnels, with their toothpaste-white
Tiled walls and their rocket-launch echoes.
As I'm always a bit slow when it comes to
Public transport, I had to ask this Irish couple
If I was waiting for the correct train coming.
They indeed confirmed that I was in the right place.
So I said to them, "Thanks. I'm always a bit
Of a numpty when I'm riding the metro."
And the Irish man said to me, "Oh, it's all right.
You speak English fine." And I blinked.
I didn't want to point out that I was from
Edinburgh, Scotland, as didn't wish to offend
Him, but, I suppose I was heavily bearded
At that time – and most folks don't suss me
As Scottish when they see me.
Through the oldest underground routes
In the world I flumed. I went to Hyde Park
And sat there for a while, watching the civilians
Walking their dogs, and it made me wonder
How wealthy you would have to be to live
In this metropolis; the same time as I watched

The crystalline outlines of the skyscrapers
On the horizon. Those images that bespoke
Immense wealth, international prestige.
That night I was staying with my friend who
Lived near London Bridge and so I headed
Over there, walking down towards the Thames.
It was crazy walking in that central part
Of the town where almost every street name
Had some connotation that you knew from
Hearsay or songs or culture in general.
Everywhere was famous. This was where
The plague happened, where the Great Fire
Happened, where the flames broke out;
This was where the Blitz happened.
Nearly 70% of the city was burned down
In 1666. And, during the Blitz, around
43 000 civilians were bombed and killed
By the Luftwaffe planes; which was half of
Britain's civilian toll for World War II;
Which made one in six Londoners homeless,
And destroyed at least 1.1 million houses across
The city. And yet, none of those facts had killed
London. This was the place where
Bill Shakespeare wrote, performed and directed
His plays. It was where Pete Townshend was
From, where Charles Dickens was from –
'twas a place that'd changed the world.
I got to London Bridge, and crossed it,
Watching the thick, soupy water down below,
That raced with pumping menace. Surprisingly,
The Thames wasn't in the top 100 longest
Rivers in Europe. And yet it was this complete
Brute when you looked at it, dizzily from atop
Its bridges. I reached the far side of the bridge
And headed along into the main street, and just
Then there were two flashy cars that sped by me.
As in – glitzy sports cars – and they were
Racing against each other. And one of them cracked
Into the back of the other's boot, because the
Other had 'won the race' and zoomed past him.
Their tyres ripped rubbery snarls on the road
And there was a big dent in the forerunner's boot.
It was basically a car crash. And it happened
About ten yards away from where I was on
The sidewalk. But, nothing else happened either
Than that both vehicles went tearing across

London Bridge to continue their race.
I walked on and I went into a supermarket
To buy some beers ahead of seeing my friend.
Everything I saw around the shop was way
Costlier than I was used to in Edinburgh.
But I got the beers and then I walked through
The night (this was in November, 2018) of
London, along to my friend's flat, through the
Odd mix of buildings that seemed to spar for
Space between the jostling traffic. As you
Walked you heard all kinds of languages,
And the people you passed wore a medley
Of outfits; some in suits and leather shoes,
Some in dresses and high heels, some in
Tracksuits and trainers; and all of different
Skin colours and height and weight and
Character. Nine million people crammed
Into a relatively small space, and this is
The sparky mix that you get as a result.
My friend had finished his work at 5 p.m.
And that was why I'd been wandering
About all day instead of meeting up with him
Earlier. He lived in a range of flats that
Were hard to navigate around, and in
The immediate skyline I could see the
'Shard' skyscraper, blinking in blue and red
Dots. I finally found my friend and we
Hugged in the doorway. He was from
California, and I'd met him years back
At university. We talked into the night,
And then went to a local bar, which
Was super expensive but it was also
Thrilling to be out in the metropolis in
The proper black night; it was sublime
To be here in Londinium, even though
It was scary, berserk and conglomerate, too.

PRAGUE

We went to Czechia in January, 2017.
After taking the underground into the city
We walked up the sleety steps and into
A broad white shining city, with our breath
Puffing in the air. It'd been snowing for
Days, and as we ventured into the city I kept
Slipping up every few minutes, even though
I wore these clunky boots. We were staying
In a quiet hotel that was found down this
Narrow alleyway leaned over by tall terrace
Housing. … We went exploring, and walked
Over to the Vltava and crossed one of those
Handsome bridges, that were brown coloured
And ornamental in themselves and were
Still as important now as when they were made,
Hundreds of years earlier. To put it in context:
The Charles Bridge (the famous one with the
Arches that you see if you Google 'Prague')
Is over 600 years old. And it leads up to the
Proper old town, with the castle that was built
In the 9th Century; and the St Vitus cathedral
With those gothic gnarly black spires, which,
Incidentally, took around 600 years of
Construction to be erected in what you see now.
We walked up the hill to the castle and of course
It was all merry pretty tourist land these days,
With the rainbow coloured housing and so on.
But you still had a sense of history: that this
Was a key city of central Europe, that you were
Scaling up wintry slopes that were laden with lore.
We went into a museum, along the way, that
Was about medieval torture. It wasn't my idea
To go; because I'm usually queasy about such
Historical topics. But, I found myself in there
Anyway. And, it was even queasier than I'd
Expected. So – it was a series of replicas of
Medieval weapons and apparatus, that they used
To kill people with, a few centuries back, who
Were suspected of witchcraft. And, after
Browsing around the museum floors for a while,
I kinda hoped that some of them were exaggerated
For tourist entertainment: hoped that they
Weren't real depictions of what they used to do

To people. One example was of a tall wooden
Spike, about as big as a man: that they used to
Impale the person on, from which they would
Then leave them there on the street, to die.
Another one was a huge saw that they would use
To cut from a person's groin, up to their head,
With them hanging upside down, and they would
Keep them alive long enough so that it was
As much a painful death as possible. Another was
This metal chamber which had spikes in it,
Which weren't long enough to kill you instantly,
And they would shut people inside it and lock
The doors, and never let them out. Yes: all of
It made me disturbed. I wondered whether the
Torturers even believed that the people they
Were killing were proper witches/devils, or
Whether they simply enjoyed doing such macabre
Things, with sadistic relish … Maybe a bit of
Both. … Anyway, we went up to the top of the
Hill, and then we took the cable train down the
Side of the hill, wherein, as we descended we
Could see through the windows the dotted
Bulbous star scape of Prague, with a snug
Clattering of the carriage as it trundled down
The tracks. When we alighted at the bottom
It was night time, in a purply closeness and
Real gaudy cold, now. We took one of the other
Bridges across the Vltava. And, looking down,
There were ducks moseying in the water.
Even though it was night time and well below
Zero, and despite there being icicles that clung
From the bridge, and snow all around, the ducks
Were just sitting there in the water, calmly, waiting,
Perhaps, for daylight. It made me wonder how
They managed to survive at all. Did they stay
There all night? Amazing. … We went back to
The hotel. My girl went to take a nap. And,
I did some reading on the desk nearby. I'd
Taken a Raymond Carver book (called *Elephant*)
With me on the holiday, a collection of short
Stories. They were inspiring and they made
Me want to write short stories too. At this point
In my life I hadn't had fiction published before.
I was still in my early 20s and I'd had poems
Published in the past, but no stories.
So, Carver inspired me to start composing

My own little tales, which I penned then,
In those three nights in Prague, Czechia.
One of them was influenced by a real life
Incident which happened to me when I was
Way younger, back home in Edinburgh. Very
Close to where I live. It was when I was assaulted
By a man, when I was a teenager. It was quite
A surreal, brutal moment. When this man
Thundered out of his house and ran up
To me and punched me in the face and then
Pulled my hair. I suppose you could call it
Dark suburbia. Or, better, just a thuggish assault
From a man who must've been at least 40;
Overweight, incredibly stupid, goonish: who
Was so angry with his life, and with an ego so
Threatened, that he had to go and attack a boy like
That on a random Friday morning.
That's a whole other tale. But, what got me
Thinking about it again, was that, just before
I had come to Prague, I had been home in
Edinburgh to visit my mother's home. And, as
I was out walking, on Boxing Day, I had passed
This man's house: and seen him again.
He was drinking a beer in his living room
And I could see him through the window.
And he made especial effort to glare at me
From behind the glass, in an oafish, orc-like
Manner. And, of course, the man was even older
At this point: and he was still as immature and
Aggressive as that. The assault had enraged
Me to no end … But, when I was in Czechia,
Sitting at this desk, with a pen and journal
In front of me: I thought I would just write
A story about it, as a way of getting revenge
On this horrible man, in an artistic manner.
So I started a fable, based on what happened.
And I fictionalised it a little bit. But, the basic
Content: the violent premise of the tale,
Was true, and actually occurred.
And then when I got back to Scotland,
After leaving the Czech Republic, I typed
Up the story I'd handwritten in the journal.
And then I sent it off to a publisher. And they
Accepted it and it got published!
And, so, suddenly I was a published fiction
Writer as well. This was exactly

The type of vindication that I'd been after.
Being a published writer was way cooler
Than anything that ugly, seething man had
Ever accomplished. And it made me feel
Way better about his vicious attack on me.
Fuck him. Ha. ... But, yeah: I have halcyon
Memories of Prague, as a whole. And that
Little hotel room where I penned those stories.
There was a 24 hour shop just outside where
I would go at night, and buy cigarettes
And obscure cans of beer, and I would
Smoke outside in the snowy lane. The snow
Would glow with an illumination in the
Spooky way that snow is able to do in the dark.
And it got super cold in the a.m. hours.
At one point it was –17°C. But, I've always
Liked the cold. And I loved the kaleidoscopic
Colours of the shop's lights behind me.
Again: I doubt I will ever go back to Prague.
Because it was such a magical trip, and I
Doubt whether I could top it if I returned.
But I would certainly recommend it to
Anybody else who was thinking of going.

GREECE

Every account I've written thus far about
My experiences in each country has
Been positive. In mood, I mean. [At least
I hope they've come across that way.]
My experience in Greece was very different.
But I thought I'd write about it anyway.
I went to Corfu, Greece, in the summer
Of 2017. With my old girl, who I've also
Mentioned several times so far. Basically,
As you have probably already guessed:
Our holiday in Greece was supposed to be
A relationship-saving trip; but, it signalled
The downfall of our thing. I won't bore you
With the details of the mortal romance.
I'm sure many of us have stories of
Relationships in decline. It can be rather
Like a drawn-out fever, when you know
That the bond is dying, and there is little
You can do to try and resuscitate it, and,
For some bizarre reason, you stay with
The other person, even though the deal
Is deteriorating right in front of you.
Suddenly her gold hair and green eyes
Weren't as magical anymore. Anyways.
Physically – there was nothing wrong
With Corfu. It was exquisitely beautiful.
I remember on the first night going down
To the beach, and the sun went down across
The sea, in a seismic celestial show, with
All kinds of reds and oranges, mixed with
The wispy final-clouds in the sky; it was like
Some Impressionist classic, or the climax
Of a movie, following a happy ending.
And, on the horizon you could see the
Hills from the other side of the island.
This was proper, rural Greece: and you
Could see right here why this nation had
Been a cornerstone for Western civilisation.
I had read the philosophy classics,
Of Socrates, Plato and Aristotle
In my first year at university, and loved them.
And, coupled with the splendour of these
Surroundings, I understood why those

Men were inspired to try and make sense
Of the sheer wonder of their planet:
The Grecian islands were that pretty.
But, perhaps 'rural' was the incorrect word.
Because we were basically living in a resort
For seven nights. And, I found it total Hell.
There were lots of fat, middle aged people
Walking around. And there weren't any
Museums in the nearby town. It literally
Only had a pair of supermarkets and that
Was about it. … I hung out at the pool one
Night and I got speaking to this man who
Was from Yorkshire. I was just chatting
About various things since he could speak
English as well, and we were both drinking
At the bar. I mentioned I was from Scotland.
And, he responded by saying, "Oh, yeah,
My grandfather was from Scotland. So,
I've got a bit of the Scottish poison in me
As well." I shit you not – that's what he said.
The fact that he chuckled after saying it,
As if I would take it as casual banter as well,
Was doubly unsettling. So I went back to
My room after that. … Across the week,
There, I did do a bit of writing, too.
But, man, the heat was 35 degrees, non-stop
And it was hard to concentrate on
Just about anything. There were a few rare
Moments with my old girl, when she
Was in a brighter mood. We sat by the
Pool and she told me some stories. From
Her girlhood. Not every story was cheerful,
But at least she was speaking to me, still.
She recanted one about when she was
A kid on holiday with her parents, and
She tried to jump on a floating bed in the
Pool from the poolside. And, the bed
Buckled under her and she sank right
To the bottom of the pool, in the deep end.
And, because she was only six, she didn't
Know how to swim, or get back up,
And was basically submerged in the pool
For tens of seconds, inhaling water.
Her parents hadn't noticed her fall in.
And it was only another guy, a stranger,
Who happened to notice this odd shape

Under the water. He jumped in, and lifted
Her out. She threw up chlorine pool-water
For several minutes, coughing and spluttering.
She had very nearly died. She said that
When she was underwater
She was scraping at the tiled walls of the
Pool and hollering for her mum and dad.
But they couldn't hear her.
And, it was insane to think how she might
Not be here right now, as a twenty something
Year old woman, telling me this, if it hadn't
Been for that stranger man who rescued her.
[And, I still loved her, by the way. With
Her tinkly, music-box voice, and Polish accent.
You must think me a loser to still be
Writing about her after such a long time.
I suppose that's what love does to some people.]
There aren't many other stories about Greece.
I would like to go to Athens in the future,
In order to re-try the nation. I'm sure if
I experienced it in a cultural way, I would
Dig it a lot better. From the week I spent
There, it was largely a long, heat-addled
Nightmare, full of unhappiness.
But, the supermarkets did sell really cheap,
Voluptuous fruit and vegetables. As in,
Proper foods that were grown locally.
I remember the olives and the tomatoes,
All ripe and proper. They didn't taste like
The stuff I knew from *Morrison's*
Back home – they tasted real. And I
Would go swimming in the daytimes.
And there would be tremendous thrusts
Of the waves coming inland from the sea,
That, as I floated on my back, would lift
Me up in steady half-violence. And by
The evenings my hair would be all thick
With the pure seat salt that'd gotten into
The strands. … And, do you know the whole
Irony of the holiday? I regret not making
The most of it when I was there, and
I wish I could go back in time and do things
Differently with that full week I spent there.
I suppose notions like regret can be
Important teaching methods.

BERLIN

I

The voyage to the capital of Deutschland was
The total antithesis of Greece.
I went on my own. In the January of 2019.
Berlin was perfekt, herrlich, gutaussehend, effizient.
It amazed me how a city of four million
Inhabitants could work as seamlessly as it did.
It was nothing like Paris or London (which both
Have mammoth populations as well). Rather,
Everything, from the transport, the way the
Trams and trains worked, to how the streets
Were spacious and spread out for the other
Traffic to flow through, to how the buildings
Were structured with their handsome walls,
All pointed to a sense of keen, impressive
Organisation. You might laugh, thinking
This is a cliché. But that's exactly what it was like.

II

My hostel was in Moabit. Which is pretty
Much city centre. So I could kinda walk about
And simply explore. I went down to the
Potsdamer Platz. And the skyscrapers were
Immense and the plaza teeming with a wide
Type of modernity. I've watched documentaries
About Berlin, about how it was razed to
Rubble in 1945. And one of the places I recalled
Seeing in complete ruin was this very plaza
I was standing in now, with its elite urbanity.
And, very close to where I was, was the
Führerbunker. That infamous manic whose name
We all use on an almost weekly basic, with the
Same kind of regularity that we say other
Names like Jesus Christ or, well, God himself.
He was there, here, in this very city,
Operating not even that long ago, about seven
Or eight decades back, and this was where
He dictated lifelong changes to Europe,
And the entire world, and this was where
He nipped a cyanide capsule, in a bunker,

Not too far away at all, just after giving
One to his beloved dog. And, to look at
The scenery around you now, you wouldn't
Think that any of such psychotic history
Had ever happened. All you saw was a
Well run metropolis, almost sleepy in
A post-Christmas January.

III

Speaking of World War II. And its relation
To just how close it was in historical terms:
My grandfather was a soldier in this war.
He was from Norfolk, England, and served
In the Royal Engineers. He was present during
Several countries during and after the conflict.
And, after the Allies had won in 1945, he
Was stationed in Berlin, when the city was
Still shaking from defeat and in occupied hands.
The Allied soldiers were left to clear up the
Mayhem the Nazis had caused in their own city.
One of my grandfather's tasks was to disarm
The Nazis' munitions, and the other bizarre
Collections that they had stolen from Berliners.
My grandfather and his regiment found
An abandoned stash of guns and ammunition in
A building that had seen the last battles before
The takeover. And, amongst the stash, of all
Things, was a bundle of *swords*. As in, a collection
Of rather rare and antique swords. That the
Nazi soldiers had stolen from somewhere
And kept for themselves, as if they were toys.
Granddad's superior told him to "dispose"
Of the swords and guns. And so, not knowing
What else to do, Granddad took the bundles
Down to the river Spree, which was close
To where they made the discovery. And he
Simply hurled the contents off into the water.
They all sank, with their weight. ... And, I
Often wonder whether those antique swords
Are still there on the riverbed of the Spree,
Somewhere? And, actually: I did go down to
The Spree myself, and cycled along it, and it
Made me feel close to my grandfather, with
This sense of lost mystery.

[Just as an extra story. My Grandfather was
Positioned on the outskirts of Berlin, in the
Aftermath of the war. In Spandau Prison.
He was a prison guard. That was when
Albert Speer was held as an inmate, awaiting
To find out what would happen to him
After his Nazi crimes. And, it astonishes me
That this man was a close friend of the man
Mentioned ^ above, and was clearly aware
And culpable with the Final Solution, and
Yet he only served 20 years in prison for it,
And that he was eventually released, and
Afterwards was allowed to publish books.
And lots of people bought his books
Because he was allowed to write them in
Prison and because they were keen to know
What being an inner member of that fascist
Faction was actually like. Scary. Incredulous.]

IV

I took the metro over to the east side of
The city afterwards. And I went to a museum
Which showed what the Soviet side of the city
Was once like, from the mid 1940s up until the late
1980s. And, it was fascinating in a completely
Different way. Again, I've watched many
Documentaries about the Soviet Union.
And have a decent general knowledge about
The time zone, and the basics of the history,
And how Berlin was divided and so on.
But, stepping inside this museum was like
Going into a science fiction novel, or film.
Or, as if being a character in a retro videogame.
The museum would show you how
The 'standard bedroom' would look in
An East Berlin house or apartment,
In the Cold War era. And so they had the
Electronics and gear that were used back then.
And, as a 'Westerner' from Scotland, it
Was all totally different to anything I'd
Experienced before. Even the colours and
The shapes of basic things, such as
The telephones or the televisions,
Were all like an imitation of reality.

I've always thought that about the
Soviet Union: as if it never really happened
And was almost made up, or faked.
That the most surveillant, oppressive
Empire of all time was almost fictitious.
The museum went on to explain how
People were spied on. And it said that around
A hundred people were shot trying to
Breach the Berlin Wall. The Stasi had
A network of thousands of civilians
That they manipulated against each
Other in order to make arrests and monitor
Behaviour. The Cold War, like WWII,
Was in recent memory, and its effects
Were still here on the European continent.

V

I went cycling through the Tiergarten
And even though it was cold and rainy
And the trees weren't in bloom because
It was January, it was still glorious and
Among the best bike rides I can think of.

VI

Would highly encourage anybody to
Go to Berlin. It is a monumental 'feat'
Of a city. When I got back to Scotland
After I went there, I actually dreamed
About Berlin for months. You know
When you get recurring dreams? When
I slept I kept being transported back
To Berlin. And I was saddened when
I woke up, because I wasn't there anymore.
In the future, I do aim to go back.

BUDAPEST

I

This was in the early summer of 2022.
So, it was following the pandemic, which
Had changed the world and knocked off
Two years of normality. Hungary was one
Of the countries that had reopened, without
Any travel restrictions. So I got the plane
Over on my own. And there was that wondrous
Refreshing zeal of going travelling again,
After being cooped up in lockdown Scotland
For such a long time. But, of all my trips,
Budapest remains the most emotive. And,
Here are the stories why.

II

I got in late at night. It was still very hot,
With the aftermath of the day's heat. And
I wandered through the streets and drank in
Some of the bars, with the drinks dirt cheap.
The next day was stunning with sun, and I
Went out walking into the city. The Danube
Glittered and the bridges over them were as
Colourful as toy cars, colourful as spring
Flowers; and when you walked over you
Got the full gaudy span of this mighty river.
I yomped up Gellért Hill, where one had a
Panoramic view of the whole city, of two
Million people; the orange rooftops, mixed
With the endless spires, domes: that wide
Sense of grandness, of having once been
The helm of an empire. The first two days
When I walked around were just fantastic,
With the pretty gals in their summer gear,
And the atavistic trams that tumbled by
In clementine flashes. ... And, I had brought
Copies of my novels along: so I could leave
Them about the city, for folk to find and
Pick up. I left some on that hill ^, on its
Winding paths, and I left some in second hand
Book shops too: perhaps hoping I might

Start a Hungarian fanbase. Ha. [Although
I've never heard back from any Hungarians,
So I'm not sure my tactics worked. But it
Was worth a try anyway.] And I walked down
To the island part, in one of the sections of
The Danube, there they've made a whole bunch
Of kids parks, and fountains, and there were
Loads of merry folk pottering about, a real
Nice scene. And on the way I was thinking
About my elder brother and his wife, who'd
Had had a son a few years back. And I was
Literally thinking, 'I wonder if they will
Ever have another child again.' And, when
I sat down on one of the benches in the park,
I was looking at my phone, and came across
The family group chat. And Louis, my big
Brother, had literally, 30 mins earlier, shown
A picture of a new baby in Kirsty's womb.
So, he was announcing the news to us.
It was spooky as Hell, that I'd just been
Wondering about it, and here was the news!
And so, the whole holiday thus far had a
Kind of 'destiny' to it. Mind sound cheesy,
But, that's what it was like at the time.

III

I've been a fan of Beethoven my entire life.
It's hard to express how important the music
Of Ludwig Van Beethoven is to me.
Are you familiar with his biography? His
Personal story is just as inspiring as his music.
Despite all the deranged obstacles that he
Faced: he remained defiant with his art. Most
Musicians reach their peak when they're young.
Beethoven peaked in his latter years,
And only improved and improved. Which
Is astonishing considering that towards the
End of his death, he was nigh totally deaf.
Anyway. I went into the Hungarian National
Museum, and I explored inside. It was all
Very lofty and there were a whole bunch of
Things to ogle at. But, by chance, in a corner
Of one of the floors, I noticed a *piano*,
Which was in this quiet little room with

Nobody else in it. So I went inside … and read
That it was Beethoven's personal piano.
Ludwig had passed it on to Hungarian
Composer Franz Liszt after he died. Beethoven
Cherished the instrument up until he perished.
What a find, indeed. Just to think, that
You were in the presence of that great man:
Just to marvel that on this very instrument
He must have composed all that material
That I had grown up loving. And, though
His scores are often turbulent and stormy,
The piano itself was very handsome and
Kempt: it looked as if it hadn't been touched
Much. In that silent, tiny room, I was directly
In front of an artistic legend. Could feel
His power with me inside there.
[And, I actually left one of my novels
In the museum garden outside. Because
I, cheekily, and perhaps arrogantly, wanted
My own artistic creation to be near
Beethoven. Though of course we can't
Make any comparisons between either man.]

IV

When I go to different countries, I usually
Make an effort to use the basics of the
Local language. Hello and thank you, etc.
Just to be polite. I should have been a bit
More prudent in going to Hungary, as the
Local folks don't tend to speak English that
Fluently. Not that this is a criticism whatsoever:
Because I'm not fluent in any other language
Myself. And I probably sound like an
Idiot whenever I try even the basics in
Another tongue. But, anyway, on one
Of the days I was there, I went into a
Café, looking for something to eat. I'd
Noticed on the chalk Menu outside that
They sold Vegan stuff. There was this older
Chap at the counter, who must've been in his
50s or so. So I greeted him and asked him
If he had a "Vegan sandwich?" And, he
Blinked, and couldn't understand what
I was saying. He kinda fumbled about,

Pointing at various items that were around
The shop, whilst trading a few lines of
Broken English. It went on for about
Two minutes, whereby he just didn't
Get what I was saying. So, after several
Times of trying to ask for a vegan sandwich,
He finally deduced the word 'vegetarian' ...
And then he offered me a can of sweetcorn.
I politely declined, and left. I said, "It's okay,
Thanks anyway, it's okay," and I exited the café.
He wasn't offended or anything, and he
Didn't seem to find the incident mortifying.
So I doubt he was bothered by the incident. But,
Yep, that was about the funniest moment of
Language barrier clumsiness I've been
Involved with in my life. Though I guess
It was pretty much my fault. Folks often can't
Understand me in Scotland, when I'm speaking
English, so, hey ho.

V

Holidays can change in mood, very drastically.
I guess, because, you're in an unfamiliar place.
Home is a gargantuan number of miles away,
And on a different island from this continent.
You are far, far away from home. And, therefore
It leaves you a bit vulnerable. And so, with the
Above stories, everything in Budapest that I'd
Experienced had been joyous and I was having
A blast. And then, on the third night whilst
I was there, a person who I hadn't spoken to
In years suddenly got in touch with me. And,
It totally changed the arc of the journey. And
Sent me tumbling with a whole load of emotions
That I'd never addressed before.

VI

I've never quite been able to deal with grief.
I tend to just block it off, when it happens. I
Suppose it's a type of defence mechanism,
Because I can't deal with the emotional content.

VII

My old girl. The one that I've mentioned before
Throughout this book. Who I went to Poland
With, and to Cyprus with, and to Prague and Greece.
She got in touch with me when I was in Budapest.
Suddenly there were messages in that old conversation
Box that I used to know daily, that used to be a part
Of my everyday life. And yet, it hadn't been alive for
Four and a half years. I went back to my hostel
Room and I called her. And, then, her music-box
Voice was there again in my ears and mind. And
We spoke for a long time. She had gone back to
Lodz after moving away from Scotland. And,
I'd actually been thinking about her the other day
On the aeroplane when I came to Budapest:
Because I'd gone on so many trips across
Europe with her, the noise of the plane brought
Back those memories of her. And, here
She was, still alive, and speaking to me.
There were many things I'd wanted to
Ask her throughout those four years of
Absence, and now I was asking them.
I suppose the main thing I had to address
Was that she had fallen out of love with me,
Long ago, and that, though she was still alive,
That love was never coming back. And, to
Hear her voice again was exotic, and also
As sore and aching as anything I've known
In terms of mental anguish. It was just so
Hard to hear that little sound with the
Polish inflection, returned to my audio again.
And, ashamedly, I got angry towards the
End of the call. And in a petulant manner,
I hung up on her. Then went to sleep for
A few hours. When I woke up I felt awful
About doing that: and I messaged her and
Apologised. She accepted the apology and
Said that she would be fine with keeping
In touch in the future. Which we have done,
Now and then, since then.

VIII

33

But in my dazed state – the day after that
Call, I was still plastered in misery and a
Heartbreak that I hadn't been able to process
For 4½ years. Jesus. So, the first few days
In Hungary had been idyllic, and suddenly
I felt distraught, and didn't have a clue what
To do about it. And, thus, I decided to get
Spectacularly drunk. From the morning onwards.
I went down to the supermarket and loaded up
On cheap beer and just tanned in to them with
Full gusto, whilst walking along the Danube,
Following the current. I listened to the Beatles
A lot. You know when you're on holiday
And you can have certain songs that you
Get addicted to, that reminds you forever after
About the place? Well, I kept listening to
'Here Comes the Sun'. And, in between the
Songs and the walking and feverish drinking
I kept crying melodramatically. I don't know
Whether anybody noticed my red face and
Wet cheeks, but they probably did. Anyway.
I'd been walking until the afternoon. And
I realised that I hadn't peed in quite some time.
So I looked about for a toilet. Or, some woody
Place where I could pee secretly. But, I couldn't
Find any. I went to a tram stop to see if I
Could scoot back to my hostel. But the
Information was all in Hungarian and I
Couldn't comprehend it. So, I decided to
Yomp back to my hostel on foot, confident
That I would make it. But I had also
Underestimated how far I had come, on a walk
Along the second longest river in Europe.
And, my bladder was simultaneously straining
Under the exercise, alongside the building angst
That a strong urge to piss can do to your brain.
So, I walked on and on, all cramped up and
Desperately hoping that I would get back in time,
Sweating and overcome with an animalistic
Need. And, I actually did make it back to
My hostel. I got in through the front doors and
I got into my hostel room. But … umm, I
Didn't make it into the toilet. And, I just
Pissed myself. Pissed my pants. Jeans, rather.
First time I'd lost control of my bladder since
I was about seven years old. This was when

I was at the age of 29. And so I'd hit rock bottom.
I took my jeans off and cleaned up the piss,
And I slept for a few hours. It was rather
Galling at the time: because I hadn't
Brought an extra pair of jeans with me.
But, it was properly cathartic. And, just funny.

IX

Early the next morning I was even more
Upset when I went to the airport to go home,
And I couldn't stop crying, and the tears
Spilled down my face and I didn't care
Whether anybody noticed or not.

X

When I got back to Edinburgh, and off the bus
On Princes Street back from the airport, I looked up
At the castle and the sooty brickwork of the old town,
And I felt blessed that this was my home city.
Where I was born. Edinburgh was a great city too.

PART TWO – NATIONS IN THE NOW

LISBON

Rumble of the jets; holler out to Europe's multicolour: that hazy
Ease of pink and blue and the buildings forever set in still paintings,
A shrugged sense of beauty; a flung canvass in masonry and ore.
Yomp across the hilly roads and catch the cigarette funk and the
Nonchalant ladies with their small coffees and inscrutable eyes.
The flags and the bedding and the soccer scarves hang from the
Balconies in silhouette, even if it's raining, and when it rains here
It's white and hot and relentless and impervious to keen jackets …
Wherein under the collar you sweat and you taste the salt on your
Lips and rub off the drips from the forehead and mutter to yourself.
Other folks watch you with your verbal ticks and astray bodily-manner.
'They probably think that I'm mentally ill,' as you strafe around
In golden tourist district, a burst of pigeons making you flinch;
Some angry driver honks at you: this car whipping right by you
(almost killing you) as you took a stupid step off of the main path.
Here and there there's a cheer or a gasp or a round of cheery clapping.
Famous football tournament's on and everybody's peeking at the
Green neon blaze of the TV screens with the dotty men jumping
Around in shorts and taking these missionary blasts at goal.
Rank smells of meat and fish and the oil and ten metres down the
Street the oranges and pears and grapes in their gaping gory baskets.
There's a flash in your head and you remember something from the
Past even though the past has no relevance to the present 'now'.
Your skull twitches and it's another of those manic ticks and nobody
Has seen it [this time] because you're in a silent part of the street.
Hop unto a tiny café that does sandwiches and you buy one:
The waitress has thick black hair and is probably better at speaking
English than you are and she's pleasant and fair and you wished
You could have that same natural tonality with strangers,
And you say the word for thanks in her language and she smiles
Because it sounds silly but she still appreciates the effort.
You leave a tip and you leave the café and as you embark again
The sky's a shade darker and there's this dodgy pain under your
Right ribcage and you schedule the ominous sign for another day.
You pass a 'beggar' on the street, in the inner district, and she only
Has one hand – literally – her left hand has been amputated below
The wrist and you give her some coins and her other hand
Trembles as you pop them down to her & she fumbles a thankyou back.
Past this woman who you'll never see again you bounce past these
Corporate coffeeshops and designer clothes stores with their
Pornographic logos and in between them all in the street is this
Fountain with marble fairies or tiny gods or cherubs or whatever they are.
Beyond this bit there's a free museum about retro sport and you head

Inside and you're the only person there: and witness all these wacky
Photos from the Twentieth Century, with all their lost glamour and woe.
You kinda get why people love sports heroes and you know that
Maybe you're not that talented yourself and it's most likely that people
Will never adore you in that same way: you won't be awarded with
Silverware or even a wacky accolade. Won't appear on celluloid.
There's that depressive mentality coming back, you realise,
As you take a next turn in the street and in the mega distance
You see the big red bridge that you saw on the plane coming over
And it's illegal to walk over the structure because it's so fuckin huge.
Still looks pretty though and you watch it for a while as you sip the bottle.
(You sneeze and the mucus goes all over your hooker's green hooded top.
Then spend twenty seconds worrying whether anyone saw it and another
Thirty seconds wiping it off and away and you quit the tissue in the next bin.)
Graffiti in stark maroon on top of the bin and you don't know its meaning.
Next bit is one of those tinkly ministores that always look like Christmas.
Go in there and bag some oranges and peanut butter and bread and these
Wooden knives and you trade a few words with the smiley guy at the counter.
He gets that you're a tourist and he doesn't mind and is interested in where
You're from: and you make a wee joke about how "my country isn't good
Enough to be in the World Cup," and he chuckles and as I'm leaving he offers
A handshake and his fingers are warm and mellow and tough and it's
Only men that shake hands like that, out of a timid desperation.
Back to the hostel. Going up the stairs there are all these pops and pangs
From the other folks living there, playing music, or these couples arguing;
Aftershave & alcohol & tobacco & the old scent of the carpets underfoot.
You pick some slices of the bread out from the loaf and you take up the
Knives as well and you slather the brown paste on them and you chomp and swirl.
(There's no lamp or chair or desk or mirror in the room and there are these
Countless marks on the walls from past embattlements, these streaks on the paint.)
Alone. Now. In a foreign hostel. Head out to the balcony and open the doors.
A handsome fifty metre drop down below and it would be so easy to climb
Off the railings and just jump ... "But no I'm not veering towards illness!"
It's a natural vibe to have when expressed at high volume, tall height.
By this point there was an apricot glow in the sky and the home city
Was readying up for the game that they were in, in twenty mins' time.
Across the balcony I heard this man and woman yelling at each other.
Couldn't fathom a slice of the vocabulary but it still sounded astonishing.

MILAN

[Part I]

Fairy lights in the windows of the high rises blink in rainbow neon.
You head out in the dark morning to the Metro and the city's on
That edgy verge of wakefulness, a sun waiting to burst.
The station is all filmic colour and windy echoes and the balletic
Language sparks about in small quips that you don't understand.
Unto the rushing tunnels and the ringing tannoid voice overhead.
Up the stone steps and met with the whispery air, raindrops
Licking the cheeks and hair and shining the routes of the trams.
You walk by a cathedral that's 500 years old and you graze
The same earth that all those people enveloped that long back.
This is a wonder and you are your own unit and mind.
Magazine stalls pop and ping in pink and yellows with their
Startled postcard shacks and magnets and soccer tops agleam.
The words on the newspapers are all stark and sound amazing
And you wished you were learned enough to write and read them.
Onwards through these streets with the drizzled lamps, the hushed
Pigeons flocking and the tram cables in black athletic arrows above.
Cough, snarl, roar, grumble, go the trams, buses and bikes.
You were headed to this particular museum but there's an
Angry sign outside saying that it's closed so you take a left turn
And head into this church that's right next to it and go in through
These seismic oak doors and whence inside the lush airy magic
Of the realm is mixed with the little pots of glowing candles and the
Sheer span of the ceiling and the all-time glory of the lofty paintings.
You don't dare breathe loudly in such a place and walk at a calmer pace.
When back outside you pick up the volume and take a new route.
Cafés begin to open up with orange windows and the chance smells
Of warm pastry and coffee and through the windows there are
Young folks with aprons scurrying about with bravery and youth.
Beyond these are the fruit markets with the gaudy botanical shapes
And the gizmo markets with the weird array of antique and souvenir,
All this electric garble and then fancy hats, hoodies and snazzy sneakers.
As you venture, all these balconies gaze down at you from fifty, sixty
Feet and there are often folks dabbling upon them, smoking & shouting.
The architecture just seems the stuff dreams are made on and you
Could be a nobody or anybody versus that calibre of creation.
You take a newbie direction. To this other museum but it's too busy.
Then bounce down the street and you ponder where else to go.
Then your phone dies and you did have a back up plan in case this
Happened which was to charge it up from the laptop – but you forgot
To bring the cable with you and now you gotta head all the way back

Without Mr Phone – you silly boyo – a rookie mistake.
You get to the underground again after asking a pair of gals where to go.
And eventually reach the district where the hostel is, and it's pelting rain
Pretty hard when you get off and you think you're going the right
Way but you finally get lost and are totally clueless, and you need
Some help from another person, and see a Pharmacy on the street corner.
And so you dip in there and it's almost pitch-silent inside and
There's this young woman at the counter with these hard glasses
That sit nicely over her delicate face, over the ears, above the blonde hair.
You explain what's happened and she offers you a charger.
"You can stay inside the shop until it's done, it's okay," she says
And the voice is lyrically kind and clean and you thank her,
And crawl down by this plug socket in the corner of this random
Chemist and you wait for your telephone to come back to life …
As you wait there are other chaps that enter the store and they're
Sick or they have troubles and they talk to the counter girl
And again you hear that piano dialogue dancing around.
You wait until your battery had a chance of survival maps-wise.
And until the girl has served the other customers and you
Thank her in her own language and you honestly are grateful
And it gives you a bit of spirit to know that most people
Are goodly-hearted, if there's the chance to help out a stranger.
She accepts the gratitude, and then she goes, "You can take
An umbrella as well," and then she takes this umbrella up
From the corner of the room, "because somebody forgot it. Your
Hair is all wet. You could do with it!" She smiled. He thanked
Her again as he was leaving. Grazie Grazie Grazie Grazie.

[Part II]

Ladies with liquorice eyelashes go tick tock on the cobblestones.
A church clangs the time in handsome gold reverb in the blue air.
Some ex colleague comes to the joint and there are big handshakes
And those manly hugs only men do and then that crackly language.
Voluptuous shapes of fish dart and sting in the canal water whilst
Overhead on the bridges these strangers pose in colour for cameras.
Stalls stuffed with glitter globes and metal toys with famous flags.

Yonder down the park there's a Christmas fair, a week unto 2023.
Kids go crazy on the carts and bumper rides in mock violence
And it kinda makes you wanna be a child again, that your body
Were that small so it could fit in one of the lil carriages in glee.
The leaves lie in wet auburn triangles on the floor and the adult
Folks smoking leave these terminal white puffs in rangy sight.
On the stereo speakers are these age-old Xmas classics sang in

American English with their universal crooner spleen and ore.

Out from the market and unto the lofty streets with the vermillion
Trams shackling by as if it were 100 years back and you
Were in a movie or a photograph and weren't anybody magic.
You pass the Farmacia signs with their seductive green neon crosses.
There's a Poste Italia – here – and you pop in there, with a postcard
You must send back to your father in the United Kingdom and
The office inside is very hushed and the ladies in the booths are
Senior and wear gaudy paint on their eyes and there are a few words
Of English as they look for a stamp to send the card airborne …
Grazie you say as you leave and there's a Polizia car outside;
And there's a slight glimmer of nervousness at the slick blue vehicle.
(Yesterday you passed a governmental building of some sort and
There was this lady outside in camouflage uniform and this
Humungous machine gun saddled nicely in her arms as if she were
Holding a baby: and it was shit scary to be that close to a gun:
Because you've never seen one up so close and physical before.)

As you walk your memories holler about with this inner friction.
Which jumps out in these random words, talking to yourself.
You wonder when your mind will ever stop being so relentless.
But when you're in another part of the world … you feel, hmm,
A bit forgiven? Perhaps? And you'll just have to live with your
Condition – whatever indeed that means – will need to prevail.

There's the gaudy crimson M sign of the METRO and, err, let's
Go somewhere else and you yomp down these cold stairs and the
Sound changes with the texture of the oxygen and you head through
The grey tunnels with these tiled walls and citric banners con
Quelle parole folli … and then you're on the deadly space of the platform
And your train's a-coming in 3 ½ mins and you look at the indigo
Tracks and wonder how easy it'd be to jump off and wait there
With the sooty tubes and those electric bars of however many volts.
The train comes and seventy people get off, seventy go on, through
This scared bustle after the doors slide to and then there's a beep
Beep beeping to wink the need to not be in the causeway when they shut.
Then la tua fluming under the city at this insane mph speed and your
Headphones are drowned by the gushing rumble of this animal vehicle;
The windows making these flashing reflections of yourself and the
Shapes of other people – women & tots, and there's a fluffy dog – and
You all make a distance across an entire span of a two million metropolitan
Area in thirteen ticks and then there's this new station to bounce off on.

Construction! This new skyrise's being erected and there are these
Racy sounds of hammers and machinery and the windows are only frames

And have no glass and the soil around the building is all warred up in brown.

Out from this station and along the roads and you pass the graffitied walls.
These energetic symbols in wonky capital letters; slogans of masses.
Some of them are names of people and you don't know the reference,
Who he or she was and you wonder when the graffiti artists come out
To prowl: coz you never seen them spraying: only see the spray paint.
You get to this super matrix of new highrises next in hard blocks v the sky.
Wondering what the people inside the balconies are like – and many of them
Are athletic it seems, for the bicycles tied to the railings, and many are
Botanical too, for the range of plant pots with the jungle leaves wavering.

"Scusi?" there's this man that's just crossed you. Behind you, and you turn:
And take the headphones out again and he jabbers some sentences at you.
He has olive skin and these purple eyebrows and you eventually
Get that he's asking for a cigarette – sure, he can have one – and you
Pop the packet out and hand one over and he says thanks, my friend.
[Just a simple favour for somebody you've never met or will see again.]

A mini football field afterwards with these boys taking
Pops at the goals and they're wearing tops of AC Milan and Internazionale
(and still being friends despite arch rivals) and you find it odd
To be in a country where the soccer quality is actually worldclass.
You hope the lads grow up to be athletes themselves, and you wished
You could join in the game, but that'd be weird, to ask, and your
Wearing these beefy boots and you were never good at football anyway …
Farther down the street there are these posters for art museums either flank.
Neo modern art; bodies in magical forms of despair, all confused by this
Century, and you hover by the bin outside the hostel garden, finishing
A cigarette and listening to those chaps footballing in the park and
Wondering where to go afterwards and marvelling at the wealth of Europe.

[Part III]

Ultimo ballo per le strade di Milano. "Where are you from?" says the woman
With the crazy orange frizzly hair … "Take a guess?" you say, and you grin.
Can't stop grinning and she frowns and concentrates on you and you wait.
"Belgium?" she ventures, with a smile. "Scotland," you say, proudly, and she
Tells you where to put your bag and as you head down that hallway there's
This man with silver fox hair tells you how to work the locker door buttons.
Then you romp around the atrium and are met intensely with these suits of
Armour worn by medieval knights five hundred ticks back and next to that
Room there are all these rifles erectile in glass cabinets with their triggers
Tracked back and you read about which wars they were from and wherein fired.
(As if those battles were anything to be keen about and there are pictures

Depicting the soldiers too, on these hazy green fields as if it were a storybook
Or fantasy treat for the eyes, with these stickmen storming a castle, fast as ants.)
Up to the next floor on these stairs which squeeze and tremble under the boots.
Christ. On this new room – in it – Jesus Christ, the most famous man ever,
And fifteen depictions of his body razed on the cross in varied colours agleam.
It's marvellous that the image of a slain, dying body could be so influential
Across history and remains an icon in the modern glitzy age, that this man
Could have such masochistic power within the service of a painting, whether
He even meant to be so strong as that; so daring to try and be a moral person.
There's another man in the next chamber, also, with all of these arrows stuck
In his thin body, tied to a tree with pink globules oozing from the wounds.
[Saint Sebastian, made a martyr in 288 AD; but he didn't die from those bows:
He was rescued from execution initially by the Irene of Rome, and then
Later clubbed to death for insulting Diocletian (the emperor) from the bottom
Of a staircase by sticking up for his Christian values – and the emperor ordered
His body to be thrown into the common sewers … Standard medieval violence.]
Further rooms. With the china clocks and the gold watch-faces stopped at
Different times: the mood grows less aggressive and beyond those roll the
Cloudy airy shots of the nude women; the naked woman: coveted classic picture.
Then there are these less-universal, astonishing paintings of a man crying into a
Handkerchief and a sea port from the 17th century clad with ship commerce.
Hmm. And you wander through the rest of the museum and it's all cool.
Let's bounce somewhere else? You wave by to the redhead from earlier.
Out unto the hammering air and the white sky cusped with the chance of rain.

BRATISLAVA

A metallic crash through the open windows wakes you up.
Your body's all rocklike with the heat, and when you check
The clock it's 06:57 – and the traffic outside is already in
Gaudy bustle with these whooshes and shoots and bangs.
Beyond the road, though, there's a little park, filled with
Trees enjoying an amazed bloom of foliage and within their
Leaves there are birds which actually compete with the
Transport when it comes to the volume of their manic songs.
You're astonishingly dehydrated and it takes forty minutes
To get up properly, taking sips of bubbly water …
You're somebody that never has the heating on throughout
Scottish winters and the temperature hike here is quite the shock.
But you get dressed and geared up and head out walking.
This is the old town, with crackly-walled buildings in
Multicoloured paint and between them are the blood-red
Trams that pass by you with this astonishing feline agility.
On the horizon of the street is the castle and we don't really
Need to describe it, just go up and check it out. On the way
There's the cathedral and it's one of the most mammoth things
You've ever witnessed and as you walk under its main
Turret you look up and it hurts your windpipe, it's that tall.
You wonder about the folks who built this 400 years ago,
And how on earth they figured out to pull off such an
Achievement … because the cloud-white blocks of the walls
Are the size of a man's torso and any one of them would
Kill you instantly if they landed on your head … and there's
A small fantasy of what it'd be like if the tower collapsed
On you right now as its masonry came hurtling down.
You jaunt up the pathways to the castle, and sweat flumes
Down the neck and you're already soaked anyway and
You take a breather in a shady tunnel and there are a gabble
Of people behind you speaking Slovak and you like the
Thrish-thrash artillery of the language and can't decipher
A single word therein; and nor can you get the lyrics of
The buskers singing with their guitars but they're doing
Well and so you toss them a coin and bounce higher upward.
And get to the top. The castle is just sublime and you can
See out now for miles in stunned panorama; and what you
Most like are the flat rises the other side of the city: for
They seem as sultry dominoes in the sun, with a rash
Ironic beauty and there are thousands of people alive within
Them with their own characters that you know nought about.
And, halving the city – of course – is the river Danube.

Up at this height it seems enticing and you have the urge
To descend down to it and see it up close and so you do that
And choose the modern bridge over the river and it's
Rather like approaching a monster or supervillain or god.
You're familiar with the Thames and Vltava and the Spree
And Vistula ... and they're all spectacles ... but there is
Something different about the Danube. The waves lunge
Heavily as you peer down from the bridge banister and
If there was any river to drown yourself in it'd definitely be
This one; and you wonder how many people have done that
Already; and the memorabilia that lies lost and forgotten on
The riverbed – what else may people have lobbed from these
Bridges that dare to span its width; and you look across to the
Bank sides and there are no fences there and you consider
Creeping down them and feeling some of its water, just to know
That you touched the liquid of the Danube; and ponder from
Whence this brute was created and how long it took to
Become what it is today: long before mankind, that's for sure.
It passes through ten European countries and that's some effort.
Overhead, the cars hurtle by and they shudder the metal
Plates under you with giddy horror and you cross along to
The far side and come by the by on the city park and because
It's twenty six degrees Celsius a lot of the woman are wearing
Dresses or skirts and you can't help but watch their legs.
The white smooth fertile luscious contours of calf and thigh.
You're actually reading a book at the moment (written by a
Famous American author) who talks about the first time he
Goes to New York and he observes the ladies on the streets, too,
And notices their differences compared with his country roots.
So you're not the only one who does such a thing and don't
Think it leery to say so. And the park has these spurting
Fountains of angelic water and turquoise pools and now and then
There are statues of prominent Slovak men in purple stone and
You find it marvellous how a person in one nation can be
Eminent enough to have somebody else make a sculptor of them
And yet you've never heard of them and have no clue of their
Biographies and you wonder whether they'll ever be making
Statues for you personally and you conclude probably not. (Ha.)
Next, we go back across the old bridge over the Danube, and
Come to the corporate area where there are a gabble of plush
Skyscrapers in silver and navy blue gleam and it's like a mini
Island of finance with these fat logos of companies above their
Revolving doors and you feel out of place there – like you'll
Never be working in such a tower or field of mass business.
And beyond that edge of the city are other towers in construction;
With men in fluorescent yellow and orange and helmets

Working with hammers and ropes hundreds of feet up and
The other ones smoking cigarettes in their vans beneath.
The roads are ragged here and you've kinda gotten lost a bit
So you find your way back into the old town, and by now its
Midafternoon and the sunshine shows no signs of relenting.
There's the national gallery with its pillars, and afterwards
The main square which is about as ancient as anything here;
And dotted around its shape, the embassies of Japan, France,
Spain, Italia, Polska, Czechia and Slovenia: right in the hub
Of geopolitical bodywork: and their flags seem half out of place
And a quarter bold and another quarter internationally proud:
And, aside most of them is the starry flag of the European Union;
The sad irony being that there's a Union Jack flag at one point too.
You pass a church with a pretty spire and head nearer to see if it's
Open; it's not, and you decide to head back to the hostel for a while.
They say there will be thunderstorms tonight, because rain's on its way.
Good. You always liked thunder'n'lightning. You look forward
To the break of humidity and those other sounds rampaging the citadel.

VALENCIA

On the horizon a gleam of late clouds lie,
perfect as shapes of ice. This is the least
colourful place to be seen all day and yet:
it's the Mediterranean Sea.
That touchdown of commerce.
The Sea that made empires, and Europe,
and this nation.
White shoots froth against the
blue vastness in these regular waves.
What'd it be like to swim out there and
just keep swimming and never return?

Smells of diesel from the beach-worker chaps;
girls walking in bikinis: men with flatter chests
than most folks: the insectile cranes from the
port on the horizon. Viscous seagulls snapping
at the bins. This gigantic cruise ship, scarily huge,
lain beyond the coastline,
bespeaking of offkey wealth and
noir novels from the past.

A swim in the sea would be nice, but, the wallet
and jeans and backpack getting stolen wouldn't
be so pleasant. So it's not so keen to leave your
bag here whilst you dip unto that watery vessel,
no matter how glorious it is.

So, let's head back into the city.

Pots of paint explode everywhere. On the walls
and down the alleyways and the walls of the parks,
there are pictures and paintings of all kinds.
Skulls and beasts, witches and dames;
mad wolves and fine cats.

All of these artists made all of this street art so
long ago and you know none of their names
and that seems the greatest point of art,
within any medium.
[Many of the buildings in this district are
smashed up or abandoned with this gnarly
masonry tumbled between their
deserted courtyards.]

Flags of lemon, tomato and blue on the
balconies overhead.
Pigeons meddle in bred crumbs
in the 28°C degree shade.

A walk in the market, perhaps?
Market building's like a train station
except better in terms of glassy width.
Intense smells of fish and meat.
And there are hacked-off limbs of cows,
and so on, and those slivers of the fillets
lying there in the shelves. Not so good.
But the olives, courgettes, peppers,
watermelons, nectarines, strawberries,
berries and nuts and bananas are all terrific …
alongside the gaudy homely smell
of the bread section.
When you buy a baguette it's warm
under the paper. And, an orange as well?
Spanish orange. Vitamin explosion.

Out onto the regular street beyond
the famous market. Sit on a bench.
Peel the orange skin apart.
A man comes up. He doesn't speak
the same language. Money.
That's what he's after. May as well
give him some. Why not? The man is
obviously mucked up; it's okay to be
charitable in a tiny way.

The cathedral plonks out its bells.
Sings them, rather. These orchestral clongs
of metal resounding over the city – and it's
not near the hour or related to the time of day.
But the sounds are railing and one could be,
if you think of it, alive three hundred years back,
to close the eyes and listen to the echoes
throughout the spanning courtyard.

How about the central park which cuts
through the centre of the city, next?
Palm trees make iconic silhouettes with the sky.
Pure camera candy. Angelic fountains of aqua blue
followed by young folks cycling in whizzing sparks.
Are they trying to get fit? Or do they do this every day?

There are hunky men, further down the park,
doing lift-ups and their biceps are pumping.
And, farther ahead, there are the green
squares of the football, basketball and tennis courts.
And, again, it is odd being in a country where sport
is far more flagrant and possible than one's home one.
(Because you see the badges and scarves
and identity all over town).
The tip tap and crack and of their young feet
going on the astonishing green span of the
Velcro pitch: wouldn't it be nice to go and
play with them, even if the mutual skills aren't there?

The karate-like language bangs about
in the hot air. Sexy language, no doubt:
hard to emulate. The purple in the flowers
of the trees that you pass doesn't look like purple;
looks like some other colour. But the trunks
of the other trees are so bulbous and twisty
that you imagine climbing up them
if you were a tad younger.

Try somewhere else in the city. A metro ride.
Stupid fumbling about with the ticket machine,
trying to get a ticket, with these other
people waiting behind.
Watching the other faces on the train (whence on it)
it's not like being an individual: rather feel like
a nobody man on a planet with eight billion people on it.
But, this is okay, only a natural feeling?

Going through the black tunnels of the Metro line,
the lanes of the train corridor twitch in lime green
and they wind and turn around the underground matrix.
There are men with grey hair. Women with wrinkly skin.
Groups of boys with brown skin.
They look at their watches and there is a wonder
what there personalities are like,
and yet there is no way to know them ...
and then after five minutes later they will
get off the train and ... there is no cinematic conclusion.

Getting off the subway and walking up
the steps into the startling sunlight.
Perhaps head down to the Fine Arts Museum?

It's free. Sounds cool.
Most of it's religious art. Almost all.
And it's astonishing how violent that
type of art is, despite how white and pink
the skin of the protagonists. The stories on the
little placards where they describe the
gory details of said Saint or Hero.

These images are totally different from
the street art you witnessed earlier.
And yet it seems valuable to wonder
why religion and sacrifice
still remains important in the present age.

Outside of the museum, the city
booms and ticks, still. The gulls circle and
meander overhead. Walking back towards
the hostel, and passing a park, there are
three black cats, coiling there,
beyond the bars of a fence.
Their eyes cut up with feline verve.

By the last tilt of the day the sky has changed
and some glimmering clouds are left, with a
sad fruity sunset beyond the hills.

Against this backdrop the neon lights of the
towns beyond the city have emboldened up,
and they wink and twinkle in
tiny distant dots impossible to touch.

PARIS

[Part I]

Spill upwards and out into the air,
Span across the length of the nation.
Clouds ease by in brilliant white cotton shapes,
Making you wish you were a giant and could touch them,
The way there's that urge to burst a
Bubble you see flying near you, or that
Instinct to catch a floating feather.

Mind that it's only just morning – with that
Fresh colour in the sky like waters of remote streams ...
And it is quite a stunning thing to be alive
And such moments as these make you feel a
Different person, or rather
You tend to forget the woe that often bothers you.

Is that *London*! To see the metropolis from such
A height, and the Thames so tiny, the skyscrapers
These little dominoes or like pieces
In a Monopoly game; and you
Imagine or recall how cramped and manic
That city is with its nine million inhabitants
And from this range it's a mini boardgame.
And then the plane goes onwards to the very
South of the UK and you know the map,
The shape of the country
Having seen it on paper or screens so often, but,
Here you can see that final triangle in
Brazen array, and the sea chasing the ivory cliffs.

In not too long a time we're over the fields of
Europe.
A special kind of grace ... to observe the green and
Brown squares and their fringes of verdigris trees.

The plane descends and goes into the clouds
And there is nothing but rushing mist beyond the windows.

These open up into the stark mechanical buildings
Outside of the city; and when the plane arrives
There's a thumping satisfying jolt on the runway.

Then the bustle and confusion of the airport with two
Thousand other people mostly all feeling
Befuddled as well.
But you get the train tickets to take you
Unto the citadel
And it really wasn't that tricky
And the airport workers who help you
Out probably find you ditsy and so they should.

Anyway, let's bounce.
The announcer on the speakers proclaims
Each name of the station as you prevail;
You always thought that the sound of the
French language was half balletic and half rash.
And yet the English language would be totally
Different if it weren't for the French.

There's a stop nearer to your hotel but you
Decide to get off further down in the most-famous
Part of town, as to your introduction to France.
That uber cathedral that springs up in international
Knowledge very oft': and, oh, there it is – after
Heading up the tunnels of the Metro and out into
The hot windy sunny space.

Siene, there is the Siene, hurtling in camouflage-green
Arteries all bashing together, and the open topped
Boats with the folks on board snapping shots of the
Lofty alabaster buildings lining the river.
Downriver you venture; your hotel not being open
For check-in yet and so you may as well wander.

Plush restaurants each place you glance.
With flowery decorations on their signs; and as
We weave further, the cafes with their maroon canopies
Beholding TABAC, with little pools of men and women
(mostly ladies) smoking on their chairs,
With those short violent gusts of tobacco smoke
That you don't normally like back home but
You seem to get a kick out of when travelling.

The ladies wear tights and they often have thick eyebrows,
Or differently shaped jaw structures from what you're used to.
There are policemen standing in pockets with their hands on
Their hips and they talk and laugh in loud volume,
And by the by a group of workie men in orange fluorescence

That you catch a few words of as you pass.

More policemen whizz by on flashing motorcycles;
And several times there are ambulances that whoosh by
With their sirens screeching *neehnaww* in manic echoes.

You get to a certain part of the city. That second-most iconic name
(one could argue) of Paris; the bit where the first revolution
Exploded over two hundred and thirty years back.
There's a monument, nowadays, a long column, alit,
Engraved and inscribed. And, do you know, it's sealed
Off with fences taller than three men. But somebody
Has climbed over them and graffitied the monument,
With the words, 'STOP GENOCIDE' in red spray paint.

You often found the history of the French revolutions scary
And gory, and, well, that's what they were like.
Guillotines, mass public mayhem, rife public hatred.
It was ironic that they had made this monument as an
Ode to all of that uber destruction; and not passing any judgement:
It only seemed a weird thing to celebrate violence.
But, then, you'd literally just left the UK, where
It was 5th of November recently, and people were still
Fizzing fireworks four hundred years after similar
Actions in London, which hardly anybody
In the modern age knew anything about:
They were only keen on colour and gunpowder these days.

The hotel is opening soon so let's head over there.

The trees line the streets either side of the roads
In direct beneficial order and they're all mature trees
And yet seem to fit exactly well into the urban zeal of
The arena
And this is one of your favourite features about
This continent,
From each sublime city you've adventured around.

Beside the trees are clogged missions of bicycles
In lime green and lemony yellow, and you have to be
Wary of the mobile cyclists that pop and zing by you
On the pavements, also stuffed with the fat vermillion
Bins and the pigeons that waddle prettily around your shoes.

You get to the hotel. Up to reception and there are two women
There, maybe a tad younger than you. You'd thought that

It would be more formal but they just give you the keys
And then that's it and one of them smiles in that way that
Some people do well and others can't.

Up to the room where you'll live for the next three days.
It is on the top floor. And when you get inside, and after
You've taken off your bags and coat, you open the window
And look down at the sheer deathworthy drop below you,
The expanse of noisy urbanity underneath;
And if you look to the left you can see a whole quarter mile
Streak of Paris, simmering in the mega moment.

[Part II]

Let's head a walk along the Seine.

Chilly this morning; and the sky hasn't quite woken up yet.
You get to the river and go down from the cranky main road
And onto the esplanade.
This is arched over by the many bridges, old and new.
The Seine's water is grey and mucky when you see it up close.
Across the far bank side are people living in tents.
And on this side, under the bridges, are further folks,
Dazed and covered in a mix of cardboard and plastic,
Almost as if there weren't bodies within those sleeping bags.
Makes you wonder just how many people across Europe
Are homeless … and it's quite the ghastly thing to imagine.

In various moments there are locked-off holes in the main wall
Of the bank side, that, when you look through the bars,
Suggest spookiness and metal objects and masonry
That vanish off into blackness.

The sun is burgeoning a little and the clouds ushering askance.

After forty minutes you come around the wynd on route, and,
Yes – there it is – what your destination is:
That tower that pretty much anybody on the planet knows
Or will know or has known from countless films, books, television
Shows – all conjured from architectural iconography.

You're not quite close enough yet and so you yomp nearer,
Across the bridge and into the park under the tower.
And look up at it.
Within the lower innards of the tower are these intricate

Mazy stairwells that wind up and there are working men
In crimson coats needling up them in small scale.

Around the tower you go, and take some photos.

As you're holding the camera this woman approaches you.
She asks you where you're from and you tell her and she
Seems nice, and she's also holding a clipboard, and what
Happens next all happens very fast;
She claims to be from a charity for deaf children
And gets you to fill out your name and country and
Several details on the paper she's holding and the pen
She gave you and you ask her what this is for?
And you don't quite think this is right; it seems a bit
Fishy and so you don't put your proper details on the
Page as you don't want to sign up for things that
You don't fully comprehend.
Oh – and then she asks for a donation.

Money. She's after money.
She might be working for a charity. But might not be.
You remember a similar scam in a tourist area in Milan,
Where these guys would force a bracelet on your wrist,
Without you asking, and then they would ask for money.
I.e., that's the way they make a living, and it's not
Particularly honest.

"Oh, you didn't say that at the start," you say, a little embittered,
But you give her a coin anyway.
And then head off.
And moments later there's this ping at your legs,
Accompanied by the woman hissing "Oh, that's *crazy*."
She's just thrown the coin back at you, and when you
Turn around, she has stormed away.

You pick up the coin. Put it back in your wallet. And head on.

Get the Metro back to your hotel.
Odd how a hotel in a foreign city you'll only know for
A few days can exude the sense of *home*.

Need some groceries for later. So you bout out down to the shop.
The store you chose last time was a bit expensive so you
Figure to try a new one this time farther down the street.
And get there and go in.
You wander about inside for a while and because it's

A new joint you don't know where everything is.
So it takes you a while but you eventually go to the counter.

Where a clerk is serving other folks in a fumbling fashion.

He looks at you as you bring the items before him, and keeps
The stare there. And you've always found it hard to be looked
At – or to meet other people's eyes – as natural shyness has
Been a part of your life your entire life.

But you just hand over the Euros for the items.

He's saying something to you in French so you say "Sorry?"
And then he mumbles some English.
He points to your backpack.
You don't get what he means.
Until he says, "Can I see inside?"
And you just think *oh for Christ's sake*.
You open your backpack and show him the empty
Bag inside it … because that's why you brought
An empty backpack to the shop: to fill it with food.

"Sorry," he says. And then he completes the transaction.

He thought you were stealing.

You wonder why a person such as yourself would
Give off the vibe of a thief …
And it's hard not to get angry when people suspect you of such things.
But it's often better to avoid confrontation and just prove that
You didn't steal anything, and perhaps make the other person
See that they're in the wrong.
At the same time: when he apologised, he wasn't sorry at all.

Fuck it. Let's go home.

On that walk home you get shat on by a pigeon.
Shit you not – that's what happened;
After that dodgy lady next to the Eiffel Tower
And this clerk who has just searched you in a supermarket:
This Parisian pigeon decides to take a shit on you, plopping
Its liquidy white poop on you from a hundred yards above.

You feel it with a hard plop on your back.
Taking the coat off, the mess is quite impressive.
Wipe it off with tissues.

At least this third incident is quite funny.

Back to the hotel. Relax for a while.
When the evening comes, you figure
to head to a different part. Northwards.
Where there's a canal that arrows through the city.
As you go, Paris reminds you very much of London;
That similar notion of intensely cramped population;
With so many people whizzing about at once:
And you really have to keep careful with the thrashing traffic.

On the way, you happen to pass the Bataclan.
Which you know only from those insane attacks that happened
Eight years earlier, almost to the week.
Now, the venue is only that, with the doormen standing outside,
Chatting to each other.
It's a mad thing to think that on this spot there happened
A sublime murderous event and that now there are no signs
Of that at all … and you imagine that, 8 years ago, on that manic night
This whole part of the city would be cordoned off,
Or teeming with running people, police cars, ambulances.

The canal is nice. Yes, sure; and it's sunset time now
And the pink light plays across the area.
On the little bridges that cross the canal are
Love padlocks
(is that what you call them?)
Clung to the railings.
Left by young fanatical naïve lovers in the past.

Getting dark, so let's return to the hotel.

Those ambulance sirens again …
That wailing seesaw noise jouncing in the overhead volume.
This is quite the racy metropolis indeed.
Tired, tonight.
Get some sleep in and we can explore elsewhere
In the daylight tomorrow.

[Part III]

Down the street there's a famous cemetery.

Waking up in the young morning you decide to go there.

It's not that far a walk.
The graveyard is clamped off from the modern world;
Walled off, literally: but, when you head in there it's like
Jumping back a couple of centuries.

Each person has his or her own tremendous tomb.
Small little houses of stone, pretty, bleak and with moss
Growing atop their rooftops, and often with stained
Glass within their interiors, with Latin and French
Words inscribed in the stone alongside the religious references.

The leaves of the trees are scattered or fluttering or
Lilting along the path as you venture,
Landing in your hair or making pirouettes on the pathways
In the November breeze.
Oh, and all in auburn and wine reds and sad yellows.

First on your radar is Marcel Proust's gravestone and you find
It, and it's a handsome tomb, of black, with his name in gold
Lettering across its front, and, there are flowers lain atop it –
Fresh flowers – and it must be exceptional to have somebody come
To your burial place so long after your death, to leave you flowers.
[What *you* say, to Marcel, is, 'Thanks Marcel, for the influence,
And rest in peace, sir.']

Buried in the same yard is Oscar Wilde.
When you get to his grave, the masonry is fenced off with plastic.
And there's a sign on it from the council saying
'PLEASE DO NOT DO ANYTHING SILLY AROUND THIS
GRAVESTONE BECAUSE IF THERE IS ANY DAMAGE DONE
TO IT THEN THE FAMILY WILL HAVE TO PAY FOR THE REPAIRS.'

But there are bouquets left under the plastic fences, too.
That's Oscar Wilde ...
His skeleton is underneath you. A chilling magical morbid feeling.

You compliment Oscar for his words, as well, and then you bounce
Elsewhere along the cemetery.

There are elder women placing flowers around the gravestones;
In that curt placid hardworking way that older ladies labour.

Next on the list is the lead singer of The Doors.
When you get there his tomb is completely incongruous to all that
You've witnessed thus far ... for it is properly sealed off with
Metal gates, and the pipes of them are plastered with multicoloured

Stickers, tacky and out of place and belonging to a lost modernity.
There's a photo of him. Flowers, as well. [You were never that
Into the Doors, but, the intro to *Apocalypse Now* remains among
Your favourite movie sequences.]
And it is bizarre how a rock musician seems to hold such an impress
Over other artists, other people in general ...
Marcel's tomb was totally different.
What is it about popular music that makes people so swoony?
Just a question, observation.

Okay let's venture somewhere else.

When you leave the graveyard – Paris and its rapping pulse come back,
And you're suddenly back in the veins of it again.

Where next?
Down to the botanical gardens
Across the other side of the Seine.
The Seine seems cross and not to be messed with and you feel
Careful as you travail the bridge.

The early winter has made dormant much of the botanical slots, but,
There are various evergreen trees from perplexing parts
Of the world that are still here and in full bloom and some of them
Are mighty spectacles far far older than yourself: if one of their limbs
Were to be cut off it would kill you in an instant if you stood underneath.

At the end of the gardens you reach the streets once more,
And turn a different way,
And come across a campus of one of Paris' universities.
There are many young folks spilling about, with their budding faces
Perched upwards, speaking in mini rings that you have no part of.
Makes you envious to not be that age anymore; with that stab of nostalgia
From your own student days that occurred so long ago.
But – good luck to them, bright chaps: you wish them well!

Back to the hotel.

As you go up the stairwell, the cleaning lady is doing the laundry
And the floors and the bin bags all at once, and she also works
With a manic intensity and you step over the bags and bounce up the
Tired carpets that line the stairs;
And think about what this building used to be: because it's an old
Place and was obviously not always a hotel;
And the room you have now is small and right in the city centre
And thus you think of who might have lived here back in time.

The hotel is ace, though; you really dig its atavistic quality.

Charge the phone up for a while inside your room.

Then head out into the addictive streets again.
Without much destination. Just wander.

The raw smells of coffee from the cafés,
And the ladies sitting under them with the wide eyeliner;
The shining pastry shops with their golden bread and croissants,
Where well dressed people move articulately inside;
The gaudy funk from the cheese shops and the grizzly
Slabs of meat, the dead animal in slippery plastic.
Then the chocolate shops with their exquisitely priced
Squares of cocoa and sugar displayed like wedding rings in the
Window frames;
Next to the niche shops that sell fancy electric lights;
Or a place that offers antique clocks; or this joint selling French
Paperbacks with brown pages that you wish you had the knowhow
To read; or these gnarly laundry joints with trundling machine machines
And women sitting under them gossiping about who knows what;
Or sandwich cafes with these sweating baguettes through the glass
With tired lettuce and tomato, and dead pigs and cows.

There are a few dots of rain.
It said on the weather report earlier that it was supposed to be
Raining heavily by now; but predictions of the weather are
As inaccurate and chaotic as anything else.

You get back to your hotel again.
The stairs smell like chlorine and they ping pong with echoes and
There's a lady wanting to go down whilst you up,
So you pause and let her pass.
Merci. She says. Merci, you say.

COPENHAGEN

[Part I]

Flying across the North Sea you come across these
knife-like islands ragged against the water; blustery
and cold looking: and they make you think of those
violent men who bustled in boats a thousand years
back, seeking new land on new coasts,
determined for spoils. Much of the language you speak
is down to them, and now you're coming
Here a thousand years later, all numbed-eared
from aerodynamics, all spoiled with the sights of clouds
from such a height as the Vikings could never see ...
And so, let's explore this new country and see what happens.

It's an early flight and so the airport is super quiet
upon arrival. Doesn't seem like an airport, only an
airy space with folks wandering around.
But, when you get to the Border gates,
and meet a woman with black hair
Through the strong window glass, she goes,
"Why are you in Denmark?"
In quite a blunt manner. But you play the civilian:
"I'm just a tourist.
Back on Wednesday." She asks you if you're
with somebody and you say
No it's only me.

You get the metro into the city. There is always
something profound about entering another nation
when you walk up from the concrete
Metro steps and into the light, width and wind
of a novel town. You come out onto a square
500 yards in breadth and pockmarked with
Pigeons and layered with cobblestones and centred
with a fountain brimming
In blue and white. You sit on one of the benches.
The winds really
Are quite nippy and they flap your hood.

There are five hours until your hotel opens for reception
and so you fancy a wander to kill some time.
Off you go walking to see what's what.

Starlings explode from the rooftops in
shotgun fodder ballet, soundlessly,
And then disappear again overhead.
There are lots of gulls, too, keen on
The fish fodder from the restaurants;
that acidic biting smell of fried fish
From the restaurant tables outside –
with the tent plastic flapping overhead.

You go into a shop and buy some things
and it's super expensive, far more than
expected, and a young woman serves you
and she giggles a little
At your locational ignorance in making the
payment, how to handle
These bizarre coins.

You head south. Towards the canal district.
The sun expands the green water and it alights
the housing from the eighteenth
Century along the straights of the esplanade
in pink blue yellow green & gold.
Like walking alongside postcard vanity in real time.
The boats, too, hang above
The half fairy / half murky water. They don't quite
have a purpose aside from to
Float there in touch maritime vibe: with the wrist-thick
brown ropes tied to the steel rings by the sidewalk.
And their names in RAINBOW CAPITAL LETTERS,
Gleaned across their fronts and sides.
You don't see anybody in their hulls and
The seagulls perch above their masts and
twitch and observe the humans fluttering by.

You head out of the tourist district and
into the south of the city, going along these
Skinny spans of sea, and you wonder what it
would be like to fall in the water.
There are no fences or walls above the drop,
and you ponder how many folks have
Fallen in the past – how many stories there are about that …

You look across the watery spans and in the
distance you see the industrial area of
Copenhagen, with these tall tunnels erect against the sky,
churning hard smoke. And, before those, a quarter mile away,

are the navy boats. These Goliath military
Ships, proper war material. Except, ironically,
when you see them for the first time
They look like they're coloured in those *Airfix* paints
that you used to colour in
Plastic soldiers when you were a boy:
they have that same toyish tinge of grey,
That seems to distract from their size and power ...

Stopping by another bench nearby, you sit there for a bit.
Some man in his fifties or so comes up to a bike
which is stationed close to the bench.
He says something in Danish that you don't understand, but you
Figure if he's asking if this is your bike?
So you respond, no, politely.

Bikes.
You'd heard Copenhagen was a 'Bicycle City'. But, Jeepers.
The bikes clog up the roads in a clunky manner and yet they
glitter effortlessly
In the sun in their metallic paint; and they suffocate each street
you meet and yet they keep breathing at the same time:
and the cyclists aren't fast or
Manic or aggressive like they are in other places: they're just
Everywhere. Young women on bikes; boys biking with headphones;
older women without helmets gliding along:
older men with cigarettes from their lips, pedalling.
[Makes you want to hire a bike as well to enjoy the experience
and get with the programme, but, you have a few bad memories
with cycling and kinda retired half a decade ago.]

Your hotel should be opening soon.
So you head back north towards the location.
As you go you pass lots of jogging folks as well.
Most of them are female.
And you watch the shapes of their bodies,
of their faces, in ripe milliseconds.
When you do get to the hotel,
the reception lady is Spanish. Brown hair, eyes,
Skin: she was speaking in that elastic language
with somebody else when you
Entered. She gives you the keys to your door.
At this point you've been awake for
Way over a day. An absence of sleep distorts
your thinking. When you get into your
Room, a great tiredness goes over you.

And you eat a little bread and humous
Before heading onward. And down the corridor
of the hotel room you can hear the
Voices of the other residents, too.
There are further Spanish girls. And some of them
Are Polish. Some Danish and some from England.
A whole mix of nationalities.

Shall get some sleep in for now. And explore further tomorrow.

[Part II]

When you wake up you hear the tinny
spidery voices of the girls again
Down the hotel corridor. You like the noises,
though they make you lonely;
You'll never translate what they just said,
and yet, the sounds of the tongues
Are brilliant. Up, you get, hot and dehydrated.
The bottled water doesn't taste
Like water as you slug it down.

What shall we do today? Let's head up to
The military fort, surrounded by water:
sounds wacky, intriguing.
When you get outside the air is white and
brittle and the flags alongside the
Canal side vibrate in the breeze.
You turn west, taking a new road, turning
Grimy, and loud, with native men in their vehicles
and fluorescent work clothes,
Repairing the roads with their tools, yammering
back and forth in Danish and smoking cigarettes,
drinking steamy foam-cups of coffee. Ordinary men,
non-tourists, starting their day jobs. At the end of the
street is some gargantuan building
Resembling something like a mammoth white tent,
with a jumbo logo MAERSK on the flank side. As you
venture you hear an apocalyptic boom booming of some
Kind of machinery that actually scares you even
though you're on civilian land.
As you pass there are innocent stalls with magnets
and glitter globes; and dotted by these are the seafood
cafés, wherein, through the back windows you see
The young folks gearing the kitchen up for the long

dreary shifts ahead.

They've turned what used to be the army fort
into a tourist attraction: though
There are still army folks that reside there.
Nearby the premise there is a museum
Of the Danish Resistance Movement,
from World War Two. And close by it
The statue of a man holding a stone rifle
in weatherbeaten cyan, looking crestfallen.
It's crazy how often this particular war
crops up in Europe. And, how you can
Feel the aftermath of the Nazis even in a
barren oceanic place such as this.
Seventy five years back those rancid tyrants
would have been here, marring these
Very docks … But it's also a fair thing to know
that there were men & women
Who stood up to those fiends. Even if it took
other powers to fully end their fantasy.
You walk through the park, where the blossom trees
are in confetti pink against the straights of water which
reflect the grey clouds a few miles upwards.
On the far distance are the other hulking factories
with their chimneys and rapt echoes.
You get to the famous *Den lille Havfrue* statue,
stranded on a boulder a few metres
Above the water height. It's a tiny affair, and nice ornament.
And though it's early in the morning, is already surrounded
by folks snapping pics on their phones.
Good to know that literary icons still inspire attraction.
Even though the Fairy Tales that we all know are as mucked up
and perverse and violent
As anything else can be in global storytelling.

Stuck on the banisters
Nearby the statue are all kinds of stickers in a meddly of pop art;
a range of rock bands and music venues up town and there are
soccer badges and motifs of social movements too.
You head on from the Little Mermaid and come across
This other statue, of a nude woman nursing her baby.
You don't know the story there.
Is it a monument for the woman, or her infant?
The name on the front of it doesn't
Connect with you. Onwards you go, climbing up the hills of the park.
Inside the hills there is a hexagonical moat. And, on the side of it,

an Anglican church that, as you approach, ding dangs out the clanky
Tune when the Hour strikes on point.
The building is half depressed and half handsome in the sombre light.
And by the kirkyards and slinking onto the moat water are these tall willow
Trees that draipse their branches into the mini abyss in quiet drowning.
There is a willow that grows aslant the brook, indeed.
Though you doubt Ophelia will be making much appearances
in tourist land, except perhaps
By night and when the castle lands have closed down.

Atop the mounds of the fort you can see out for some distance across this
End of the city. And then one of those navy ships hurtles down the port water.
The sailors scurry about the flanks of the vessel in minature mania.
You go to take a short film of the boat on your phone bit it moves real fast
And your lens doesn't capture the focus well enough. Hey ho.
Walking down to the land-fort, you pass another group of soldiers.
They're holding real guns. You really don't know anything about guns
Aside from in movies, and it's always tantalising when you're that close
To them in the flesh. The soldiers are babyfaced and
probably younger than you are ... but, they're all clad
in camoflague, and hold these weapons,
And so you get a little prickly by being near them,
and you head out of the security gates, expecting some
kind of dodgy thing to happen to you.
Alls well, though, and you exit safe and then head
back into the city. A few times, at length on the horizon,
you've seen the dome of a church
In pulsating note, a handful of times. So you reckon you'll
head over there to see if you can go in. Along the streets,
the cyclists fizzle by, and the sun
Comes up in brief spurts of loud yellow, and you get to the
church in short time and, yes, you are allowed to go in.
Many other folks have had the same
Idea as you, and when you enter the atrium there are maybe
thirty folks scattered about the long benches leading up to the podium,
and all under the planetarium-like dome reaching apwards 200 ft.
Watercolour artwork and alabaster masonry align the perfectly
circular walls, and you marvel over the skills of the people
who made this place so long ago.
And what's more wondrous is how hushed thirty strangers in a huge
Room can be when inside the vicinity of a mighty church – for – you
Can barely hear anything save the silent ticking wonder of the crowd,
Spanning their eyes around the innards of the dome.
Seems like religion
Still has a little relevance, in terms of peace, amidst the wrath
and confusion of the modern age across the globe.

A building to respect. You leave after a
Short while. And head out exploring unto another district of the town.

[Part III]

A bout to the cemetery the other side
of the island is the morning plan.
Sunny day. Buoyant sanguine Spring sunshine
that pangs off the canal
Water and sparkles that and sparkles
the bikes stacked up in their hundreds
By the streets as you dally. You need a
fridge magnet for going back home.
Heading off into the hub of the city centre
looking for a souvenir store you
Pass the corporate shops with the famous
international names. On broad
Windows are splashed the adverts for
cosmetics and perfume with these
Supermodels pouting their pulpy lips.
And unfortunately there are the
Fast food branches with their sickly logos,
mixed in with the fashion stores,
The shoe shops with their lady leather boots
erectile through the screens.
On each restaurant MENU that you pass
it's all either meat or fish.
The coins are a bit confusing in Denmark
and when you find a magnet you
Give the girl at the counter too much change.

After the store you head into this new park
with a little lake inside it
All amazed by the light of the sky,
simmering in pure reflections.
Swans and ducks mosey about,
about as careless as water birds can be.
You come out of the park and onto the bridge
that crosses the main canal
Leading off the island and on the brinks of the
bridge are the bloody flags
Of Denmark again. Shortly after the crossing
you come upon a basketball
Court. Surrounded by buildings
smothered in graffiti. The courts of the

Playing field make you wish you had a ball
to bounce there, to throw up
At those lurking orange rings … and you can't
discern much of the graffiti
Letters on the walls, nor understand the artwork
spattered between the
Raw inscriptions, but they work in the
rash urban zeal of the scene.
The scenery quickly changes into
a charming district of florists, bakeries,
Bike hire shops, ice cream parlours.
Shame you can't really appreciate
Any of the cuisine, for personal ethical reasons (ha).

In close time you reach the cemetery.
Hans Christen Andersen is buried there.
It is odd how a field full of
Skeletons underneath the soil can attract
so many alive people a day.
Free of charge you can go and see the tombs
of dead folks and maybe
Tingle at the nuance of their bones
under the flowers and grass that
Align their patches. Above Hans' tombstone
they've put daffodils and tulips, looking like
any Easter Card decoration. Born in 1805,
Died in 1875. Snow queens, angels, goblins,
elves, storks, teapots and ugly ducklings
don't seem to have anything to do with this pretty
Graveyard. But it gives you a bit of momentum,
a bit of inspiration, to try and have achieved
something before you perish yourself.
Maybe try and do something before you die
to perhaps have your own
Bones nestle in a similar place somewhere
on this sublime continent?

You figure you might try a museum next.
And there's a castle along
The way so you can see that too.
Heading along in that direction you come
across a bunch of kids
Out playing on the street.
Are they high school kids? They play
With basketballs and footballs and they
shriek and shout with that inner

Value of youth. It's a week day after all
and so they must be on their
Lunch break from the school. Do you wish
you were as young as them? Not really because
you remember the agony of adolescence.
And yet, these days when you look across
at the car reflections in Europe
You see your white hair and your tired face
and you're always on your
Own and thus you don't really feel young anymore:
and all the folks in the hotels you stay in are either
way younger than you or far older,
And thus you don't seem to belong to
a particular age bracket.
But, meh, oh well, whatever.
You're still alive and that's what counts.

On the upper scores of the buildings
are random chunks of letters
That resemble steampunk videogames
from the 1990s, or graphic novels
From the 1980s: and it's remarkable how
those concepts will have influenced
Such phenomena in modernity, right there,
illegally splayed on the roofs
Of the city centre houses.

You get to the castle. There are spikey gates
in front of a long meadow
Leading up to the building. In the foreground
of the fortress are a band of soldiers in boots
and fancy hats, playing music.
A big brass band.
Pumping out crowd-pleasers
with their fat drums,
trumpets and blushed faces.
They seem to be performing to nobody
in particular save the gabble
Of tourists picking photos from 200 yards away.
But they still do the music pretty well.
Have to hand it to them.

The other side of the street there are a couple
of Danish men getting drunk
On one of the benches. They drink from
green cans and have sweaty faces

And the bigger man sings something
to you as you pass. Not intimidating,
Though: only merry rather than offensive.

Okay so here's the museum. History museum.
With a mix of cultural and artistic
Regalia from within Denmark and across
Europe and northern Africa.
There are respectable ladies at Reception.

They give you a key to stack your bag,
and then you head upstairs, going to
The top floor. As you ascend, the
 light diminishes and all grows dark, and
As you head unto the showrooms,
it's like being a kid again going on a school
Trip, when you're in a new environment,
and it's humid and there are these
Glass boxes blooming in the darkness.

Maps, diagrams, histories of warfare,
Ancient coins, ancient knives and pistols.
They're all real and so you wonder
Whether they ever killed anybody.
There's a whole region dedicated to
Islamic history. The empires that ranged across
An entire spread of two continents,
that spanned between Spain and Persia.
And so you read the snippets of writing
under each display. They all seem to
Acknowledge violence as
the key cursor for history?

When you go downstairs you see the other floors.
They are filled with Danish
Pottery, in milky whites and blue, these china pots
and plates that you would
Fear dropping on the floor if you ever held them.

Whilst you're walking
About, a woman with a museum uniform on
comes and asks you to tie your
Coat around your waist.
"Okay, that's fine," you say.
You explore the rest
Of the floors.

Then you figure to head back to the hotel.

Whence outside of the museum the clouds
have overtaken the sky and there
Seems premonition in the grey dyes of them.
Head back to the hotel for just now
and perhaps another walk later on tonight?

THE END

These poems were coined between November 2022 and May 2024. 'Countries from Memory' was written from retrospect in Edinburgh, whereas 'Nations in the Now' was written whilst living in each respective country thus described.

Best Wishes,
Harrison Abbott. July 2024.

OTHER BOOKS BY HARRISON ABBOTT

FILIPPO'S GAME

A teenager, Henry Fowles, goes missing from a leafy suburb in the summer of 1998. His body is never found and his case turns cold. He's forgotten about. Until Dolina returns to the suburb twenty years later. She grew up here and knew Henry when she was a little girl. As an adult, she goes exploring in the woods where the neighbourhood kids used to play. And by sheer chance finds a shocking clue connected to Henry's disappearance.

This involves 'Filippo's Game' – a series of secret puzzles set up inside the woods, made up of ladders, tunnels and dens. Filippo was the nickname of her cousin who also once lived here. After this discovery she wonders whether the old gang back in the 1990s may have had something to do with Henry's vanishing. Dolina is now the only one left in the neighbourhood of that original gang. Henry was an odd boy, and disliked by the others. Are there more secrets to be found in the woods? She goes on a quest to find out.

Filippo's Game is mystery novel that explores the power of memory and the dark possibilities of childhood.

A promising young athlete, Oliver Porteous, gets kidnapped one evening in the estate. Men wearing masks jump out of a van and capture him and take him down to the forest. Where they kneecap him. And end his career: he'll never play again.

Days later, Wallace 'Waldo' Holm gets a call from somebody in the estate, who tells him the story. Asking him to come back and help. Wallace used to live in the neighbourhood: but he moved away a long while ago. When Wallace lived there, the residents would go to him if they had a problem. Because they couldn't speak to the police. He was the infamous *Waldo* – somebody who could do you a favour if you needed something gnarly done.

Wallace decides to return. Mostly because he knew the Porteous family and is furious about Oliver. He also knows that he's far older now. He thought his own violent history was all in the past. And he doesn't *need* to return. So why does he agree? Just to be Waldo for one last time?

A TRADE OF GRACE

There's an economic crash. Like no other before it. And the city plunges into rioting and looting, which the authorities fail to control. Many civilians evacuate their homes in order to flee the violence. Those that do stay are plagued by mass food shortages, which only fuels the mad situation.

Four characters are still there in the metropolis, a month after the crash hits. The riots have spread to where they live and they have no other choice than to escape. They come from totally different backgrounds and have never met each other; Marvin (a man), Elisa (a little girl), Anthony Burton (an old man) and Ruby-Rose (a young woman).

There is no public transport, are no functioning shops, nothing for this quartet to go to for practical help. They're alone and must improvise. The other people that remain lurking in the city are abandoned and starving, and know that they can do anything without fear of reprimand from the law.

A Trade of Grace is a suspense novel which explores themes of survival, kindness and the dubious nature of the innocent when faced with threat.

LITTLE WATERFALL

Ralph Ballard, a solitary ex-athlete in his forties, receives a surreal phone call one morning. His brother and sister in law have died in a car crash.

Ralph's young nephew, Caspar, was in the car as well. But he survives the accident. Caspar is then placed into the guardianship of his uncle, who he barely knows. Ralph, in turn, has never had kids himself and knows nothing about children. Now he must raise a distraught orphan all by himself.

Little Waterfall explores familial dysfunction and selfishness, en route to the process of grief and redemption.

The police invade the estate and force a mass evacuation of its residents. A group of young men and boys form a resistance army and annex the local mall. They build camps in the huge forest behind the estate, where the police dare not go, and use them as bases to co-ordinate the war effort. Out-matched on arms by the police, they conjure ways in which to retaliate and defend against a thuggish authority which has plagued their neighbourhood for decades. Chronic is the sense of threat. The police, they all know, are capable of anything. The estate is forgotten by the city: the young soldiers are alone and despised by many. Angered that the army have taken control of the mall, the police plan a counter attack. Both sides gear up for a great battle. *Amazed Gloom* is part war novel, part boyhood drama, chase thriller and study of oppression.

1983. There is a mighty storm. A young boy, Leonard Hill, finds a body in Boxbush Woods. The storm buckles the riverbank in the forest and he discovers the skeleton of a girl who was buried there. She must've been his age when she was murdered.

Leonard calls the police. And they take over the investigation. The authorities peg the murder on a man who was sent to prison for child abuse years ago. Except, they cannot prove it, because he committed suicide whilst in jail.

At ten years old, Leonard is too young to become involved with the case. But the discovery of the body puts a hook in him. The girl he found disappeared from Boxbush in 1967. If it was this suspect that killed her, why did the police miss him so easily back then? Was it really him that did it?

Jason Cheever, 28, lives in the aftermath of the pandemic when the economy is still reeling. He gets laid off from his job, and bizarrely manages to break his finger later the same day.

These are the practical problems. But other cognitive issues are returning – things which he thought he'd defeated in the past. He had many incidents of sleepwalking in childhood. And now as a man, he finds himself waking up on the street, at night, with no clue how he got there. His auditory hallucinations are making a comeback too. They're getting worse. Far spookier. Why are they reappearing at this point in his life?

Jason's an artist; or at least tries to be. When he gets troubled he tends to churn out the drawings and paintings. This autumn his methods are turning increasingly erratic, to the point where he can't be sure whether his creativity is in any way healthy.

Fox and the Birch Trees is a stream of consciousness novel which explores paranoia, self-destruction and a slow loss of reality within an artistic mind.

Meet Lukas, a famer who develops an obsession for a scarecrow on his dead father's fields. Meet Mr Hare: a bitter piano teacher outmatched by a schoolboy prodigy. Then there's Paul Giggs, the autistic kid who's fantastic at his college coursework, but it looks like he might fail his oral presentation at the end of term. An elderly veteran remembers a battle in Holland, 1944, still plagued by the ghost of the man he killed there. A wealthy model has his face freakishly scarred in a car crash, and the injury ends his career. A foreign correspondent meets a famous dictator for the first time, naively thinking she has the verve to take him on. Alongside 94 other little tales.

"*One Hundred Ticks* is a collection of skilfully crafted vignettes. I couldn't stop reading as each story left me wanting more. Abbott transports the reader through a myriad of situations with well observed characters. There's something in here for everyone." – Spike Munro.

MAGPIE GLEN

Come down to Magpie Glen, a leafy suburb isolated from the city. An unlucky family called the Greenes move there looking for a new chapter in life. It seems a wonderful place to live. Lots of charismatic neighbours within a friendly community.

But their new next-door neighbour, Floyd Lennon, is a reclusive old man who was long ago shunned by the neighbourhood. And rumours suggest he's building something in the nearby woods. Hammering can be heard from his shed and there are chronic burning smells from his garden. The local kids are keen to discover what Lennon's up to. The Greenes have no way of knowing why he was rejected in the past.

Magpie Glen is a gothic portrait of suburban secrecy, conformity and crime.

POLLY'S DREAMS

Polly, a young woman with Asperger's syndrome, heads back to her hometown after her girlhood cat dies. The trip seems innocent. She and her Dad bury the cat in the garden. But after looking through old family photographs Polly makes an uneasy discovery. She is in the image, but can't remember the photo being taken, and the content is a giant contradiction. It connects with a great phobia she's had all her life. Gradually she realises that a whole chunk of memory is missing from her youth. And as she investigates further, more unnerving signs follow ... Come across the other side of the city, where a man is locked inside a mental institution. He has been here since a teenager and there is no chance of him ever getting out. The guards routinely beat him up. He knew Polly when she was a girl and often thinks about her. But does she remember him? Polly's Dreams is a commentary on traumatic violence and how authorities deal with individuals who they deem as mentally ill.

Printed in Great Britain
by Amazon

51437875R00050